CHRISTOPHER LOWELL'S **SEVEN** **LAYERS** OF **ORGANIZATION**

How to mentally, physically, and spiritually purge your home in ten days.

"The seven layers of organization are designed to help you look clearly at what you have, what you really use, and what you don't use."

CHRISTOPHER LOWELL'S **SEVEN LAYERS OF ORGANIZATION**

UNCLUTTER YOUR **HOME,** UNCLUTTER YOUR **LIFE**

Clarkson Potter/Publishers
New York

Photographs by Douglas Hill

Copyright © 2005 by Christopher Lowell Enterprises, LLC

All rights reserved.
Published in the United States by Clarkson Potter/Publishers, an imprint of the
Crown Publishing Group, a division of Random House, Inc., New York.
www.crownpublishing.com
www.clarksonpotter.com

Clarkson N. Potter is a trademark and Potter and colophon are registered
trademarks of Random House, Inc.

Library of Congress Cataloging-in-Publication Data
Lowell, Christopher.
    Christopher Lowell's seven layers of organization: unclutter your home,
unclutter your life / Christopher Lowell. — 1st ed.
    Includes index.
    1. Storage in the home.   2. House cleaning.   I. Title: Seven layers of
organization.   II. Title: Unclutter your home, unclutter your life.   III. Title.
    TX309.L69   2005
    648'.8—dc22   2004026643

ISBN 1-4000-8240-4

Printed in China

Design by Caitlin Daniels Israel

10   9   8   7   6   5   4   3   2   1

First Edition

TO MY FATHER, HENRY LOWELL MADDEN

Artist, master craftsman, moviemaker, raconteur—to this day, my father excels in everything he sets his mind to. This remarkable Renaissance man, with the soul of a poet and the mind of da Vinci, infused our home with creativity—so much so that a show of creativity was mandated from every member of the household. Over heaps of my mother's amazing Italian food, lively and challenging debate filled the dinner hour. At six in the morning, I could hear my father's table saw ripping into a sheet of lumber out in his shop. By his potbellied stove, with the music of Crosby, Stills & Nash jamming in the background, I'd watch his hands as he carved a rosette in an elaborate frieze of an eighteenth-century-style door pediment. It would soon grace one of the historical mansions of Strawberry Bank, in Portsmouth, New Hampshire, a place he would later pay homage to in a moving film for the Portsmouth Chamber of Commerce that he wrote, photographed, and edited. My sister and I gasped when the movie *The Bridges of Madison County* came out. The Clint Eastwood character, down to his very body language, was exactly like our father—except Dad's better looking. Today, his Harley-Davidson takes his free spirit across America, where—camera in hand—he continues to capture our endangered landscape and the quiet souls of the people who inhabit it. This is a man who truly has learned that he who travels lightest travels farthest.

CONTENTS

Preface   9

Introduction   12

SEVEN LAYERS OF ORGANIZATION 19

Layer One: Assess & Schedule   20

Layer Two: Detach & Purge   24

Layer Three: Reclaim & Update   32

Layer Four: Sort & Contain   44

Layer Five: Design & Build   60

Layer Six: Arrange & Display   70

Layer Seven: Cease & Maintain   86

LET'S REVIEW   92

ROOM MAKEOVERS   94

Super Studio   96

Meals on Wheels   106

Ship-to-Shore Bedroom   112

Yacht Chic Public Spaces   120

Office by Day, Guest Room by Night   126

Office Politics: Divide and Concur   130

Pass-Through Spaces: The Long Hall   136

College Cool   142

Sorority Splendor   148

Twin Toddlers   154

Retro Wow!   160

Check, Please!   166

Resources   170

Contact Information   173

Acknowledgments   174

Index   175

PREFACE

When I was young I took great pride in the fact that I had few possessions. To those who seemed to be slaves to their stuff I would preach, "He who travels lightest travels farthest." While the saying is true, some of my bravado simply masked the fact that I was as poor as a church mouse and couldn't afford fine things even if I wanted them. Expensive taste and a lack of funds kept me lean and mean through the college years. As a young adult I lived basically like a gypsy. Not only did life in the theater find me traveling the world with various productions, but I also moved a lot. By *a lot* I mean forty-three times and counting.

Moving was always my excuse to purge. Bye-bye, now! Out with the old life, in with the new. But then I got older and began investing in furniture a little at a time. I kept saying to myself, "You might need this someday." Having juggled many careers in my life, I'd accumulated hundreds of boxes filled with art supplies and portfolio pieces (just in case I had to prove I knew what I was doing). There were ten 300-page drafts of a children's novel I had written, samples of products I'd designed for clients, assorted renderings, swatches of every home interior surface known to man, and nine years' worth of design magazines. It was endless.

Then there were the boxes filled with hundreds of video-tapes I hadn't viewed since I'd directed them, accompanied by literally hundreds of scripts and endless video logs. Stuff I had no intention of ever going through, much less needing, followed me wherever I went. I actually paid to schlep this stuff from place to place around the globe, and then there it would sit in unopened boxes filling my basement, attic, office, and so on. Somehow, I suppose, keeping these bits of my past validated me. Did it give me some sort of comfort to have proof that I had created something? Why couldn't I let this stuff go? Would there come a day in my old age when I'd reflect on my life as I viewed a shampoo bottle I had created for Revlon? Long after I'd gone, would my sister's grandchildren piece together the moments of my life while watching one of my hair-care training videos? Did I keep this stuff because I thought I'd never create anything again? The questions seemed deep and over-whelming, so I kept the boxes through several more moves. "I'll think about this tomorrow," I said to myself.

Tomorrow finally came when *Interior Motives With Christopher Lowell* debuted on television to resounding success. It was then that I finally knew what I would probably be doing for the rest of my life. By now, in addition to my house and the still-unopened boxes, my retail and design studio in Chagrin Falls, Ohio, was also packed to the brim.

I made my fortieth move, this time back to Los Angeles. But the boxes did not. I vowed never to accumulate so much stuff ever again. It was time to create anew, to make new memories, to begin a new life as the home-arts guru. And create we did: thousands of room interiors filled with thousands of props, all of which had to be warehoused in no less than 50,000 square feet.

In fact, as I write this preface, my company is about to move out of our old warehouse, where we've filmed parts of my show and photographed all of the Christopher Lowell books and products you see at retail outlets across the country. You name it—lamps, accessories, furniture, walls, and windows—yep, that warehouse is crammed to the rafters. I'd done it again. I looked at Jocelyne Borys, my creative director, and we both laughed. Once more we vowed never to accumulate this much stuff ever again. So now we're smack in the middle of the biggest garage sale I've ever hosted. Our discards will now furnish a variety of charities, including Good Shepherd, a facility for battered women; Calvary Chapel; and Project Angel Food, an AIDS outreach program. Oh, and I think St. Vincent de Paul just pulled up.

Our new warehouse is only 12,000 square feet. In order to accommodate this substantial downsizing, we've put in place a system we've been working on for the past year in anticipation of the move. We've talked to hundreds of efficiency experts, professional organizers, and space planners nationwide. We've taken a look at what's available to keep us clutter free. In fact, several times we've said to one another, "There's a book in all this somewhere." But how would I condense all we'd learned about the emotional side of purging and the physical task itself?

That same question had plagued me before: How would I take everything people needed to know about decorating a room and organize it into a sequence that would keep readers focused and on budget, without overwhelming them? That book was called *Christopher Lowell's Seven Layers of Design*. Eight years later it's still a bestseller.

So we got back in touch with all the space planners, all the professional organizers, manufacturers, and retailers—even psychiatrists. We then surveyed the 2-million-plus fans who log on to our Web site each month. We asked them where the organization process broke down for them. Soon we had arrived at the seven layers of organization, and the result is this book. Believe me, it's as much for me as it is for you. Together we can unclutter our lives by uncluttering our homes. Yes, we can do it!

INTRODUCTION

We Americans are drowning in our own clutter. Our insatiable need for "things," combined with our penchant to hoard, robs quality from our lives. It's not intentional. If it were, we wouldn't do it. No one is intentionally a pack rat any more than anyone is intentionally overweight. It just seems to happen—as a result of surprisingly similar psychological needs. It's not about laziness, and it's not simply a matter of procrastination. Although laziness and procrastination eventually come into play, they're not at the root of clutter. What is, is fear. There I go again—where there's fear, there's no creativity. Fear plays with our heads and makes us feel bad about ourselves. In the posture of low self-esteem we find ourselves living in doubt. The shadow of misgivings clouds our thinking and our ability to make decisions.

Bringing order to the home is a task of clarity. Clarity must be met with determination, and determination fights the fear. Phew! Fear is sneaky. Clutter is even sneakier.

Take that nifty little blanket chest you picked up at a tag sale—when was that now? A year ago? *Gee, I could make something out of this.*

As in, Boy! With a spit polish and a coat of paint, this could really be cool. Your intentions are good, but without determination nothing actually gets done. And the longer we wait, the odds of it getting done grow smaller. And all of a sudden, you've lost credibility with the only one who counts: yourself. Whether it's fear of failure, fear of letting go, or fear of feeling stupid for buying it in the first place, fear is our nemesis.

One more time: Where there's fear, there's no creativity. This belief is at the heart of everything my amazing staff of imperfect, perfect human beings and I have been trying to convey for the past decade.

Let's review. First, we taught you how to break down the design process into seven easy layers. You said, "Hey, I get it!" Then we taught you how to identify your personal style. You said, "Hey, I'm a 'shore' person. Who knew?" We then showed you how to decorate large and small spaces from scratch. You said, "When I move out of this dump, that's exactly what I'm gonna do!" But all along the way, like a warning on a cigarette pack, we kept saying that clutter kills. Was anybody listening?

Well, yes, but by the time those words of wisdom actually sank in, a lot of us were already in too deep. Deep into crammed attics, full basements, bulging closets, stuffed drawers, cluttered kitchens, hostile kids' rooms, dysfunctional bathrooms, and embarrassing public rooms. Then there were those weird, wasted spaces that we couldn't figure out what to do with, so we filled them with more stuff. It wasn't pretty, but at least it was storage—sort of.

Should we mention the times we caved at 2:00 A.M. and ordered the had-to-have kitchen gadgets we used only once? How about the flea-market furniture that had "so much potential"? Once we got it home we realized we'd have to give up our day job to rehabilitate it. So out it went to the garage—you know, that place that was originally built for our automobiles? Then there are "thin" clothes that we

"No one is intentionally a pack rat any more than anyone is intentionally overweight."

refuse to discard just in case we wake up one morning in a twelve-year-old's body. And how about the clothes we did wear? The collars need flipping, the hems lowering, the buttons replacing, and the zippers fixing. But hey, all doable, right? Then to make things worse, there are keyboards, towers, RAMs, gigabytes, and motherboards with their billion cords and socket-robbing plugs, dot-commed right into the middle of the mess.

That's how it happens, and it happens to seven out of ten American homes. And while we've suspected this, and it gave us some sort of comfort as enablers, we still crept around the house pretending our clutter didn't exist. When asked, we blamed it on the fact that the house was too small and said we've been looking for a new place since 1977.

If you've ever looked around and wondered how your house got out of control and asked yourself where the hell all this @!#% came from, you know what an overwhelming, depressing, esteem-robbing process it is to look at your space with fresh eyes and begin again. As my preface attests, I feel your pain. So go ahead, be a big baby and take short little steps to follow me as we reenvision the home. And we're walking . . . we're walking . . .

Let's be real here—bringing order to the home does not sound nearly as fun as decorating the home. To some it sounds almost militaristic, while to others it sounds a little anal-retentive. But done properly, order is actually part of the design process—one you might have overlooked. But hey, it's never too late. There's a lot more to organizing, we found out, than simply sorting or cleaning. I've been to many houses that were filled to the rafters but clean as a whistle. I've been to apartments where everything was sorted but still packed to the gills. Organization is, in effect, a science of spatial relations combined with simple logic. So while you don't have to be creative to be organized (even though we are all inherently creative), creative organization can actually become a dramatic part of a room's overall design, as we illustrate in Room Makeovers (page 94) in the second half of this book. (Love those!)

The seven layers of organization are designed to help you look clearly at what you have, what you really use, and what you don't use—either because you plain just don't need it or because it no longer reflects who you are or who you want to be. A preview follows.

With times so rapidly changing, the way you live today may be completely different from the way you will live ten years from now. In the past decade we've learned to take buildings full of data and condense the information down to a compact disk. We can speak to anyone anywhere in the world while driving a car. We can even take pictures of ourselves while we talk to them.

We had every reason a decade ago to be suspicious of technology, even to fear it. There is undeniable proof, however, that today's technology has given us a myriad of conveniences. This does not mean, however, that sentiment, traditions, history, or folklore won't exist—they're just going to take up less room.

Purging means change, and change is hard to initiate. Technology, like it or not, has forced change upon us. Its purpose was to simplify our lives, but the downside has been the ability to multitask twenty-four hours a day, seven days a week. How much "in touch" is too much? That's probably the subject of its own book.

Meanwhile, my seven layers of organization are designed to help ease the transition from here to the near future. It's been carefully sequenced to help you survive the psychological ramifications that purging entails. But it's also a friendly wake-up call to really look at how you live. Some of this is just common sense. Given what you know about how you live today, would you rethink the home you moved into years ago? For most of us, if we're honest, the answer is yes.

You'll be surprised at how clearing the clutter from your home clears the clutter from your life and gives you the space not just to live but to *be*—to be who and what you want to be, in step with the changing times.

For some of you, organization could simply mean finding groovy ways to arrange hip and cool new things that will help you stay clutter free. We've got you covered. For you folks, you'll look at the neat pictures and check the Resources (page 170) to find out where to get the stuff we used. For the rest of you, moving to a new home might be easier than organizing your current living space. The problem is that moving isn't always an option. No worries.

"If we are how we live, then what does your home say about you?"

In Layer One, Assess & Schedule, you'll decide where you are in the process. If it's been a significant amount of time since you've really purged, there's no question this will take time. Efficiency experts say that if you're in the correct frame of mind, an average-size room can be streamlined in less than a day. So a house with two bedrooms, a living room, a family room, a kitchen, two baths, a hallway, a dining nook, an attic, and a basement will take about ten days total. This is, of course, when you're revved up and really ready to attack clutter. When I said moving might be easier, I wasn't kidding. But first you have to be realistic and motivated by a sincere desire to get your clutter under control.

Almost all of us are guilty of some form of hoarding. See if any of the following profiles fits you.

THE GUILTY GLUTTON

The most common guilty glutton is born when a loved one dies and there is an inheritance of prized possessions. I had a friend (we'll call her Judy) who had inherited a small house filled with her beloved mother's belongings. Apart from a few standout pieces, Judy admitted that none of it was her taste. Much of the noncohesive mishmash was hopelessly dated and did not suit the scale of the small bungalow it was crammed into. Judy's brothers wanted nothing but the proceeds from the sale of the house. But at the same time they didn't want her to sell anything in the house because, after all, it was their mother's and contained their cherished childhood memories. Judy also wanted to be respectful but was now stuck living in a house filled with things that did not reflect her in any way.

I intervened because it was apparent that Judy was stressing over the situation. We first went through the house and talked about the stuff. We identified which pieces could be painted a different color, which lamps might look better with new shades, which sofa could be reupholstered. This

was a useful exercise, but it wasn't addressing the real problem.

I sat Judy down and said as tenderly as I could that while I could transform any space into anything she wanted, the truth was I really didn't see Judy living there in the first place. She burst into tears. I'd hit a nerve that obviously needed hitting. She just hadn't heard anyone say it out loud. "But it's my mother's table that she lovingly polished after the Sunday meal," she sobbed. "I feel like I'm dishonoring her by not taking care of her home."

After a lot of hand-holding, I finally got Judy to agree that Mom would never have wanted her things to bring her daughter such distress. Her mother was not in the stuff she'd left behind, but in the memories of a loving relationship they'd had while she was here. But what to do with the stuff?

Several families in the neighborhood had admired the belongings of Judy's mom. So we decided that whatever any neighbors and friends wanted, they could have. Let her mother spread a lot of joy to those who really could use the furniture. Whether Judy kept the house or not, it would still be cheaper to update the interior without the unwanted furniture in it. Then, when the house was painted and remodeled for resale, if Judy decided she loved it, she could move back in.

THE APPROPRIATE APPROPRIATOR

This applies to people who, fearing the wrath of an in-law or a close friend, accept offerings they don't want and then feel obliged to display them when the appropriate person comes over. Now, I'm all for keeping the peace, and a few knick-knacks disguised with proper display tactics won't hurt anybody. But if this cycle goes on too long, it becomes a form of control through fear or guilt. In-laws can prey on your wanting to spare their feelings in order to get their own way. If you are in a new relationship, it's especially tough, and sometimes you have to grin and bear it. However, if after a few years it's still happening, then you may have to take matters into your own hands. With family, in particular, it's really more about your having the courage and diplomatic wherewithal to politely declare (either openly or implicitly) what your home décor parameters are.

This has happened to me and here's how I handled it. I stated, with humor, to a few key members of my family that I was working hard to downsize and that I simply didn't want any more stuff—no matter what it was. I insinuated that I could be a bit picky about what went into my home. While I was honored by the gesture or appreciated the sentimental value the item might have, *I just didn't have anywhere to put it.* If it was an heirloom, however, that they wanted me to archive for future generations, then I would spare no expense to store it properly.

It worked every time because I paid homage to the gift and to them and was willing to put my money where my mouth was. But the underlying meaning was, "Don't look around my house every time you come over because it will not be here but rather in proper storage befitting its family importance and value." Once that was made clear, the rest was simply a matter of personal taste. If they wanted to give me something not related to the family, I suggested that a gift certificate would be foolproof and much appreciated. If they still wanted to get me a wrapped gift to open on specific occasions, then I would smile and say thank you. If the gift was something I could not use, I would either return it discreetly or give it away. However inappropriate the gift might have been, I know it was probably chosen with the best intentions, and I would not want to appear ungrateful, impolite, or, worst of all, mean-spirited.

Now, once a present is given, the giver has no control over it. To quote Miss Manners, "That is what it means *to give.*" That also means the giver has no right to inquire about a gift's whereabouts, in or out of your home. If they do have the bad manners to ask, tell them it is so dear to you, you are saving it for a special occasion. Or something. And then change the subject. But all this leads me to the next category.

THE HEARTFELT HOARDER

These are people who save everything anyone ever gave them. My Grandma Belengerri was like this. If you gave her a gift, she'd burst into tears of joy. Given her large Italian family, it wasn't long before her home became a living shrine. And yet, she never complained that her house was

All this...

...fits here!

out of control. It would never be in *Better Homes and Gardens*, but it's what she wanted to look at, and that was that.

Not all heartfelt hoarders feel that way. Some of you do just what my grandmother did, but then roll your eyes and make excuses for the clutter. While you feel a sentimental connection to these things, you still want a designer-quality home. You just have no idea what to do with the stuff.

The truth is, if you love these things, then educate your-

self as to how best to display them. This can entail shadow boxing, framing, and finding furniture designed specifically for these purposes, as we show you in the second half of this book.

THE KEEP-IT-TILL-I-READ-IT PACK RAT

These people are characteristically voracious readers. But because of their "need to know" mentality, they allow newspapers, coupons, magazines, old mail, and everything else to clutter every surface and stuff every basket in the house. They'd pitch it in a heartbeat, but they have to read it first. I have a client whose house I designed years ago, and to this day every time I go over, I grab a trash bag and start stuffing because I can't see the furniture through the clutter.

The key here is to purge and start again. If you haven't read by now a pile of papers that has accumulated over months, you won't. To begin, keep only the material dated that month. Take some of it with you when you're getting your hair done or standing in line somewhere or having lunch by yourself. In a month's time, when you realize the amount of time you actually have to read, you'll be more realistic about what you can read. This little exercise will help clarify your priorities while also limiting your clutter.

Because of my various functions within my business, I accumulate an enormous amount of show business papers, home magazines, financial papers, product catalogues, and so on, which I put into a large Moroccan wooden bowl in my bedroom. When it gets full, I start pitching.

With my cooking magazines, I finally realized that I could go online for any recipe at any time. Internet technology saves the day (more on this later). So I enjoy the magazines and pitch them at the end of each weekend.

If I'm getting on an airplane, I spend thirty bucks at the newsstand getting all the magazines that interest me. This helps me keep my home subscriptions to a minimum. I tear out a few things (okay, a lot) on the plane and ditch the rest.

There will still be those of you who would be happiest living in a public library. Fine. Then line your rooms with floor-to-ceiling shelves, organize everything, and be deliberate about it. If it's your thing—flaunt it.

My wooden bowl. . . . When it gets full, I start pitching.

THE HAD-TO-HAVE HOARDER

These are people who, because they don't ever know what they want, seem always to need everything. Whether it's the latest and greatest gizmo or the cleverest doodad or the solution to a problem they might have one day, they simply must have it. Home shopping networks live for you impulse shoppers. My mother bought one of those vacuum food sealers, only to realize that our family ate everything in sight so there was nothing left to store in the first place. But she refused to get rid of it because she'd spent so much time convincing my father of the gadget's indisposability. For her to throw it out would mean he was right and she was wrong. While we all fall victim to a clever sales pitch now and then, the trick is to know when you made a mistake. If you used it once and the thrill is gone, then either toss it or give it away.

THE "PERFECTLY GOOD" PACK RAT

"Perfectly good" pack rats pride themselves on their thriftiness and practical attitude. To them, everything is "practically like new," "in perfectly good shape," and "the very best in its day." It might have been a top-of-the-line butter churner, but who makes butter anymore? These are people who won't part with anything as long as it still works, pending small repairs that they never make. These are people who have a workshop who never actually set foot in it except to stash the perfectly good thing that needs a small fix that they'll never make. I call it the *Sanford and Son* mentality.

THE POSSIBILITY PROCRASTINATOR

These are folks who see creative possibilities in everything that catches their eye, from a flea-market find, to a rummage-sale treasure, to an objet d'art found in a Dumpster. While these are people whose creative imagination may see beyond an item's necessary repairs, they often underestimate the time, money, and motivation they'll need to actually get the work done. So, an object once filled with creative possibilities now takes up valuable space in the attic or garage. These forlorn and thwarted projects only become annoying examples of an inability to follow through, and who needs that?

THE TRUE SHOPAHOLIC

This is obsession taken to its highest degree. These people use shopping as an emotional fix rather than deal with the deep psychological issues that undermine the quality of their lives. I won't spend time on this because it is clearly as much of an addiction as alcoholism and should be professionally treated. If you consistently buy things you have no intention of using, you could be a shopaholic. If you or someone else has intimated you might be this way, you may want to seek counseling.

Get the overview first. If you see a little of yourself in all of these profiles, have no fear. Recognizing the situation is the first step in getting to the root of why you attract and keep clutter. Before you begin the process of getting ready to purge, read this book in its entirety. When you're finished, you will have a mental picture of how to implement the hundreds of ideas we've shown you. Beginning with the end in mind and knowing there is help all along the way are important to staying out of overwhelm. Remember, you would not have bought this book if you didn't know that clutter was getting the best of you, so that's a great big first step.

SEVEN LAYERS OF ORGANIZATION

LAYER 1

ASSESS

& SCHEDULE

In Layer One, planning a schedule and sticking to it are key. This begins with assessing the whole house, from the attic to the basement. If you're not sure you can do it alone, assess with someone who can really get into it with you—someone who takes your desire to purge seriously.

If we are how we live, then what does your home say about you? I know this sounds silly, but it really works: Walk out your front door and close it behind you. Tell yourself that you're about to walk through someone else's home—one you've never seen, belonging to someone you've never met. Your job is not simply to wander from room to room but really to ransack and snoop. Open every drawer, closet, medicine cabinet, chest, box, and bin. Look under beds, over shelves, in armoires, and through built-in cupboards. Leave no stone unturned. Your goal is to construct an idea of who lives there by using their stuff as your clue.

Organizers say the more you can emotionally detach during this assessment process, the more your stuff will reveal about you. Take approximately an hour per room. Talk out loud to yourself about what you see—the good, the bad, and the ugly. There's power in the spoken word, and it keeps denial at bay. It's also a good idea to make a few notes about what you see. Ask yourself if the way this person lives is acceptable to you.

Then put yourself in the picture. Does this home reflect the "you" you're hoping to become, or is it about the "you" who wants to change?

If it's the latter, ask yourself what's holding you back. Did you not make changes because you didn't know where to start? Didn't have time? Didn't have the money? Were afraid to start for fear you might be making a mistake? Or did you just plain not want to put in the effort?

Then ask yourself how streamlining would benefit you. Here are just a few positive answers to that question.

- It will make your home seem bigger.

- It will free up lots of space.

- It will give your spirit a huge lift.

- It will give you a chance to see what you have and what you don't need.

- It will begin a process of positive change that will translate to many other areas of your life.

- It will boost your self-esteem.

- You'll be proud to invite friends over again.

- It will feel like you moved into a brand-new place.

- It will initiate a sense of order and help stop bad housekeeping habits.

- People will admire your ability to make such a significant life change.

- Once you complete one room you'll be hooked, and streamlining will start to be fun!

- The things you finally decide to keep will have new meaning to you.

Using the one-room-per-day equation, estimate how long it will take you to purge your entire house or apartment. Then get out a calendar and block off the days you'll do each room. Stick to your schedule. It's best to do the job quickly rather than drawing it out, because you don't want to break your rhythm.

"If you haven't used something in a year, chances are you probably won't."

Dated magazines, out!

Remember, right now you're just looking and assessing. It's not about design, and don't make it so. It will only be a distraction. The design process requires an entirely different mindset that you'll shift into later as your reward, in Layer Five.

With your home truthfully assessed, don't freak out. This is a real process. As the Carpenters sang, "We've only just begun!"

While you're assessing, make notes of the following:

- Anything you have duplicates of
- Boxes or containers that you haven't looked in for more than a year
- Clothing you haven't worn in more than a year
- Projects you never finished and probably won't
- "Collections" that consist of one item
- Things that you've been meaning to toss out but haven't (duh!)
- Things that don't work and haven't for more than a year
- Things you thought you'd use but haven't
- Damaged or chipped items that you still use
- Mismatched sheets, towels, dishes, et cetera
- Electronics that are out of date and could be replaced with new, cheaper, and/or smaller multifunction models
- Decorative objects and art you once liked that are now tucked away in closets

- Gifts you don't like
- Anything that's expired, from batteries to Benadryl
- Mysterious or strange food items you either don't know why you bought or why someone gave you, but that you're never going to eat
- Things you were saving to give someone but haven't gotten around to giving yet
- Objects or furniture in places only because you thought "something ought to go there"

In making these observations, do you begin to see how you got all this crap? Um-hmm.

You may notice there is a one-year stipulation with many of the items listed. Experts say that if you haven't used something in a year, then you probably won't. That's good news, because that means it can go bye-bye. And here's more good news: Once you throw out stuff that falls into the above list, you'll gain more space!

Now give yourself a day or so to review the list and really let it sink in. And don't worry about having nothing left if you get rid of so much. Remember, the idea is to open up space for new possibilities. You're about to make room for a new and exciting life. Yippee!

Mismatched, out!

LAYER 2
DETACH
& PURGE

Now that you've assessed your clutter situation and dedicated the time to deal with it, don't chicken out. We hope the first layer gave you the opportunity to see what you really have. The second layer of organization is about deciding what you really need—and clearing out the rest. First, you detach—emotionally and physically—from your stuff. Then you purge.

Purging may be easiest to do in two rounds. Round one is getting rid of the junk. This is the stuff you know right off the bat you'll never use again or is just plain (pardon my French) crap! Round two is getting rid of the clutter. And while all junk is clutter, not all clutter is junk. It may be "perfectly good," and that's where you have to be honest about what has value and meaning in your life ... and what doesn't.

So when the going gets tough, the tough get chanting: I'm making room for a new life that brings with it new opportunities. I'm not going to settle for living with junk. I deserve better! I don't care who gave that thing to me—it's gotta go.

> "So much of purging is not giving in to your feelings but rather using your head."

By closing one door on negative "poverty" thinking, you'll open a new door to the positive "prosperity" thinking that comes with clarity, organization, and high self-esteem. Even as you begin purging just the junk, valuable space will begin to free up.

Don't worry about the harder decisions down the road. Right now, your best and most effective strategy is procuring the proper garbage bag.

And I do mean *bag*, not box. I like the ones with the drawstring handles that you can tie closed quickly and easily. Don't get bags that are see-through. Out of sight is out of mind. Once it's in the bag, it *stays* in the bag! Boxes are cumbersome and hard to cart away once they're filled. Remember, you're purging, not moving!

Think of the garbage bag as being like the garbage disposal in your kitchen sink. Once something is shoved into the big black hole, it's gone. Be impulsive. Grab the item in question, shut your eyes, and jam it into the bag. It may hurt for a second, but within an hour, you'll get into it. You'll feel exhilarated as you pick up momentum. I promise you won't regret it by the end of each day. You'll find that your gut instincts, combined with a detached attitude, will keep the job moving right along. Don't overpack the bags; you'll still need to carry them out the door!

Now, let's jump right in, shall we? Below are some rules of thumb for your most common clutter items.

NEWSPAPERS

If it is more than a month old, out it goes for sure. If there are articles you're dying to read, do it online. Most major newspapers have Web sites from which you can download only the article you need and print it on to standard-size paper, which stores better than odd-shaped clippings. Better to save one clipping than the whole paper.

OLD DOCUMENTS AND TAX RECORDS

Experts say that most people save twice the number of hard copies than they need. Once you've sorted your papers down to what's manageable, there are copy centers that will scan your documents and transfer them to computer disks. An entire library can now fit into your desktop drawer, digitally preserved forever! But don't go through your papers right now; it will slow you down. Here's what I do: I put them on top of my bed each night so that I'm forced to purge them if I want to have a place to sleep. While I'm watching TV, I sort and toss. Log on to tax sites if you're nervous about throwing away tax documents and other official papers. Places like H&R Block will tell what you need to save and for how long.

TECHNOLOGY

Many people hold on to their first computer (usually a hand-me-down) and never turn it on because it's dated and nothing interfaces with it. If your fax machine doesn't work well, consider getting a fax that will also print, copy, and scan. If you have old cell phones, give them and their accessories away. If your radio only picks up AM/FM stations, get one that acts as an alarm clock and a telephone, too. Get the idea? The goal in technology is to make units smaller and multifunctional.

Chances are, if your technology is more than three years old, it's probably twice the size of what's on the market now. Today, investing in a simple and reliable computer is essential. The price you pay to be online will save you money in the long run. As the Internet becomes your shopping vehicle, it saves you time and gas. As it becomes your research center, you can get rid of dated reference books. With a

scanner, you can take those seven years of back tax records and condense them into seven disks. You can really start to see how technology can change your life. And it will, it will.

MEDICINE CABINETS

Check the expiration dates on every product and toss what is old. Chances are, a lot of what you have on hand is more than a year old and ready for the trash. If you had a rash in 1969 and still have the ointment, get rid of it. There's probably better medicine available now anyway. Yellowed Band-Aids, pill boxes with only one pill in them, night creams that you thought would make you young and didn't—toss 'em, no matter how much you paid for the promises of youth.

COSMETICS AND HAIR PRODUCTS

Experts say that most women use only three shades of eye shadow, three shades of lipstick, one mascara, foundation, and blush. So why are there 6,000 cosmetics in the drawer? Get rid of anything more than a year or two old. Shampoos and conditioners expire, too. You need one shampoo, one conditioner, and one color extender or freshener for color-treated hair. If you haven't used hairspray or mousse in a year, you won't. If it's a formal occasion, guess what? You would probably go to a professional anyway. A round brush for blow-drying and a regular hairbrush and comb are all you need. Nothing is more wonderful than getting out of a clutter-free shower and opening a well-organized drawer where everything you actually use is right there. What a great way to start the day!

LINENS

Get rid of mismatched towels in colors that no longer work with your décor. All-white everything will give your bedroom a spalike feeling and a fresh, crisp look. If you have a queen-size bed but still have four sets of double bed linens, give them to charity. If you never use the bath mat or it's fraying, toss it. Linens and towels are less expensive and of a better quality today than ever before, so replenish and upgrade when you need to. Blankets and old comforters you no longer use would be welcomed by your local homeless shelter—so share!

Display the mundane.

CLOTHING

While you'll revisit them in the next round, make your first pass through the clothes closet and the dresser. Bundle up everything you absolutely know you'll never wear again. Experts say almost half of a closet and a third of every drawer frees up during this first pass. That is, if you're really honest with yourself. Here again, detach yourself from what you were, and latch on to what you hope to be. For many, clothing is a status symbol. It's something that, in abundance, makes us feel like we've achieved something. Having a lot of clothes somehow keeps the options open whether we wear them or not. Here the "it's in perfectly good shape" mentality can haunt you. Yes, it's spotless, but *do you actually wear it?* If you haven't even tried it on in more than a year, give it away!

How would you answer these questions:

- By the time you're thin enough to wear the article of clothing again, will it still be in style?

- Are you keeping it only because of what it cost at the time? Quality clothing is nice, but useless if not worn.

- Are you keeping the article of clothing because you feel that proper alteration will make it wearable once again? While you'll have a chance one more time to update and reclaim in the next layer, start thinking about how much of your clothing actually fits into this category. I will assume that, beyond a missing button or a simple hem, the clothing in question would best be altered by a professional. But before dashing off to the tailor, do the math in terms of time and money. Is it really worth it when Target and the Gap are right around the corner? For that vintage couture dress or your grandfather's Savile Row dinner jacket, yes. For a pair of khakis or a cotton shirt, no.

KITCHEN ACCOUTREMENTS

This category deserves its own chapter, and we'll talk about it more in every layer henceforth. For now, ask yourself the following questions:

- When was the last time you made popcorn in a skillet or popcorn popper? Nowadays, the convenience of microwavable popcorn is at the touch of a button.

- How often do you use your turkey roaster? If it's once a year, get that cumbersome appliance out of the kitchen and store it in the garage or someplace where you can get to it when you need it.

- How often do you use those appliances of late-night TV fame? Did you really get as big a kick out of the Salad-Shooter and the French Fry Master as you thought you

"So much of purging is not giving in to your feelings, but rather using your head."

would? The egg poacher, the Seal-a-Meal, the omelet maker, the meat slicer, the under-cabinet can opener you never mounted? Just think of the goodwill you will share by donating these impulse buys.

- How many wooden spoons do you really need? Most chefs say four.

- How many mismatched pieces of everyday flatware do you have? A sixty-piece set of great-looking stainless is about $29.

- Do you have mismatched place mats? Toss the orphans.

- Do you have aging Tupperware? Today's disposable containers (which I reuse) come in many sizes and are dishwasher- and microwave-safe and cheap!

- Do you really use your professional cookware, or do you normally use the cheap nonstick pan because it works better? Restaurant-supply stores now sell restaurant-grade cookware; I have one oversize skillet, one frying pan, one omelet pan, one saucepan, and one stockpot. That's it!

- Do you really need to save eight empty mayonnaise jars when another one will be coming in about a week?

- How many mixing bowls do you have? Most chefs say one set of six nesting glass bowls is all you need.

- How many mismatched wineglasses do you have? A set of four is about $12.

- How often do you actually use your mother's china? If the answer is rarely, give it away or give it back.

Your home should now be littered (room by room) with junk-filled garbage bags ready to be removed from your life. Ideally, at the end of each day, it's best to get the full bags out of the house. This will prevent you from weakening and tearing them open to retrieve something you might think you still need.

So much of purging is not giving in to your feelings but rather using your head. You'll find that plain old common sense gives you plenty of reasons to purge.

By this point, your home will no doubt still be cluttered, but at least it will be junk free! What you know you'll never use is gone. And hey, there's more room than there was before—valuable feet and inches!

It's okay to have a moment of separation anxiety. It's only natural. The junk's not missing; it's dismissed. You do not need it in your "new" life. The very space of its absence is a visual reminder that change is happening. Rather than feeling loss, remind yourself that you are making your home a reflection of who you really are and who you hope to be.

Congratulations! Now go to bed! When you wake the next morning, you should be feeling the first stages of renewal. This begins the vital cleansing process that should fuel you and give you the inspiration to keep going. Okay, with the crap gone, it's time to move on.

BEFORE

AFTER

Oh gee, there's the bell. *Ding!* Round two!

The good news is you've gotten rid of a whole lot of stuff in your first round of purging. The bad news is there's still a lot left. The good news is you got rid of the junk. The bad news is that this next round of decision-making is a little trickier. It's sort of like *Survivor* but with furnishings instead of people. Your job is to begin voting the weakest objects off the island.

The objective is to determine whether you still have a positive connection with the thing in front of you. If you're honest with yourself and the answer is no, then out it goes. If it has lost meaning for you, it has no business in your home. By simple virtue of the fact that our tastes change, certain things will be easy to eliminate.

Don't get trapped in the idea that you should keep something because you have a history with it. While everything we have may indeed tell our personal story, is it telling an accurate one? If I came to your house and looked around, what would my impression of you be? Would your home, in its present condition, tell me a story about you that you'd be happy with? If the answer is no, have no fear. You can change that story.

Now, as you slug your way through this round of purging, keep the following in mind:

DON'T DO THE DOMINO THING

Let's talk a little about the domino effect. If you start moving your stuff around the room, or from room to room, but don't actually get rid of it, you're just moving stuff around. If you purge only one or two rooms versus your whole house, all the stuff you don't want in one room has a tendency to move to the next instead of out the door where it should.

Moving one pile from one room to another will exhaust you, and you'll have inadvertently initiated the domino effect. Now everything is scattered about just because you decided to move the bookcase. The bookcase is not the issue right now; it's the crap in the bookcase that should be your focus.

Purge first, to see how much room you have. Then the books, letters, and photos you do want on the dining room table can temporarily go into the bookcase that's been purged of the stuff you don't. Get it? In Layer Four, we'll address sorting and containing. But not yet! There is method in my madness.

BAG IT!

The garbage bags that you are now filling (and leaving full) should be separated into two piles, one to give away and one to toss.

"The junk's not missing; it's dismissed."

Pile One: Giveaway

These are things you will pass on to those who can use them, and by this I mean giving to charity. Of course, the very best stuff you can sell on consignment or eBay, and I won't discourage you from it, but do think it through first. By the time you go to the trouble of schlepping and/or shipping and paying the consignment shop's percentage or the eBay commission, you might be better off giving it away and taking a tax deduction.

Giving to friends is always a nice gesture, but beware because it can slow you down when you're waiting for Betty Lou to come pick up the "perfectly good" lava lamp, and she just can't seem to get there. . . . If a friend wants something, let her help you get the stuff to where you want it and cherry-pick from there. At least it will be out of your house.

Pile Two: Trash

This is stuff (along with the junk you've already purged) that should really just be taken to the dump or to the curb for trash pickup. But often this purging process requires more than that. The big stuff may need to be taken to a commercial Dumpster (which I usually sneakily hit at night) or hauled away by the professional trash guy. Every town has the guy who will remove anything at any time. Check your yellow pages under "rubbish and garbage removal" or "trash removal" and book appointments based on your purging calendar.

Let your schedule work for you.

By now, round two of the big purge should be well under way. If you schedule as I suggest in Layer One and go through one room a day, your expectations will be realistic. Some rooms may take longer, and that's okay. Obviously, the garage is a bigger job than the powder room. Your place will not look put together during this purging period, so don't worry. It's evolving and will continue to do so as long as you stay truthful with yourself. During this round, pretend that you're relocating—as long as you keep stuff moving out! Don't try to entertain or make dates with friends unless they're there to work. Take breaks when you start to feel overwhelmed.

With the house in its current condition, eat out if you can afford to so you don't have to bother with meals and cleanup.

LIVING SIMPLY IS LIVING CLEARLY

And while that sounds, well, simple, at the heart of why we hoard is a feeling that by having less, we *are* less. But living with less is better if it signifies that you've set new standards for yourself. You may have fewer belongings, but they are of a higher quality. This means that you're gaining better self-esteem. I've been in sparsely furnished homes where dramatic wall color and a few quality pieces deliberately created an atmosphere of serenity and beauty. I lived that way when I was poor, and everyone thought it was chic.

Whether the look is driven by budget or by design is irrelevant. People don't miss what they don't see, but they do remember striking spaces and whether the interiors tell an accurate story of the person they thought they knew. So don't make your budget an excuse to hang on to something you don't really want or that isn't "about you." You'll find a way to get what you want as long as you know what it is you want.

Meanwhile, get that clutter out the door as quickly as possible so you can get a clear vision of the new space you've freed up. Remind yourself that some well-deserving stranger is going to get good stuff thanks to you, and that's a good feeling.

WHAT ABOUT GARAGE SALES? While I think being able to turn your stuff into money is a good idea, sometimes it's more work than it's worth. Staging, advertising, and policing the sale could take days and might rob you of your purging momentum. The idea is to get unwanted stuff out of your space as quickly as possible. Successful purging is all about having the undesirable objects out of sight, out of mind, and fast! I've also found that people who give good garage sales do it all the time. For some it's a social thing as well. I'm not the type and you might not be, either. You decide. Remember, with donations to charity you get a tax write-off, which in my mind is as good as cash come tax time.

LAYER 3
RECLAIM
& UPDATE

Learning what to reclaim and what to update is about seeing whether the expense and effort will be worth the result. It's time to make some important choices—choices you've no doubt been putting off, which is how your clutter got out of control in the first place. And realize that some of these decisions may involve further purging. Good for you! You've developed a thicker skin and know that these choices are also about quality, the quality that you deserve. Let's get started.

TAKING STOCK

As you take stock of what you have that might, with minor changes, be updated and therefore salvageable, start with the objects—the knickknacks and whatnots—then move on to the furniture.

With your decorative objects, ask yourself these questions:

- What does this object need to make it "okay" with me again?

- If all this object needs is _____, will I really do it? What will it cost?

- If I do it, when will I do it? Within the next month? (After that, fuhgeddabowdit. It ain't gonna happen. Trust me.)

- Is it worth my time to do it? Or would it be cheaper just to buy a new one?

I swear, if you're honest and do the math, you'll likely have all the rationalization required to give the object in question the heave-ho, or to give it to someone who could really use it.

KEEPSAKE VERSUS KEEP

Now, don't get me wrong, it's absolutely okay to keep mementos, and they should be honored as long as you have a connection with them. If your daughter's baby clothes are important to you, mount them in a shadow box and hang them on the wall. Or give them to a friend who can use them. Think of how great it will feel to see a newborn in clothes you remember so fondly on your own little sweet pea.

But if the clothes are sitting in boxes in your attic, they're not telling any story, they're just taking up space. When my grandmother died I found a chest she kept in her bedroom where she had placed her mementos, much of which was clothing. Each piece was delicately wrapped in acid-free paper. Each was accompanied by a handwritten note explaining what it was and why it was special. And while the clothes were not on display, she had them close to her in her room, so she probably looked at them often. What was revealing were the thoughtful notes and the way she had honored her keepsakes by preserving them so immaculately. To me, it wasn't the stuff, it was what she did with the stuff that moved me.

It's the same with your home; it's not the stuff that needs to be valuable, but rather what you do with it that reflects your spirit and personality that has value. Your home is personal and should be treated with respect. Reclaim it as such.

BEFORE

How Do You Know If It's Worth Reclaiming?

Providing the object is not of profound sentimental value, it's otherwise all about the math.

A good lamp shade could set you back $75, on a base you thought was okay but not great. You may find a lamp with the perfect shade and a great base for $20.

By the time you have a professional slipcover made for that sofa ($300), you might find a sofa out there that's only

"Remember the equation of your new math: effort and expense versus result."

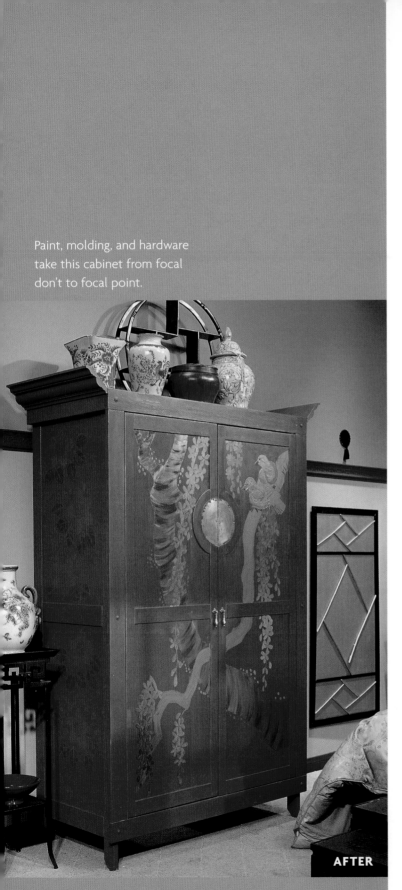

Paint, molding, and hardware take this cabinet from focal don't to focal point.

AFTER

$700 and exactly what you want. So, in essence you've got a new sofa for $400—not bad.

In the garage you may have a chest of drawers you picked up for $20. It needs repair, refinishing, and new knobs. Including your time, that could set you back about $300. Again, is it worth it? Be honest—do you actually have the time and know-how to refurbish it? Do you want to? That's even more important: distinguishing between wanting to and feeling like you *should*. This isn't about "should"; this is about "good," as in how good you'll feel when your house is clutter free and organized. So keep that in mind, wouldja?

In Room Makeovers (page 94) in the second half of this book, you'll be surprised to see how a simple coat of paint can make an old object work in a whole new way. But intentions aren't actions. You actually have to roll up your sleeves and do the work. Remember the equation of your new math: effort and expense versus result.

Some of you may have already rehabilitated a piece, but you still don't use it or don't like it. Or it just didn't turn out the way you thought it would. If it didn't work then or now, it won't work in the future. Don't hang on to something simply because of the time you've already invested in it. You can't get the time back, but you could pick up some extra space by ridding yourself of it and making room for something better to come in the near future.

FURNITURE STAYS, FURNITURE GOES

We hang on to furniture we don't like because someone gave it to us, we rescued it, or it was the best we could afford at the time. That was then, this is now. One thing hanging us up is when we say to ourselves, "Hey, it's real wood! That's gotta be worth something. I'd better keep it." Well, just because it's wood doesn't mean it's good.

A good-looking, ready-to-assemble piece that's not real wood might better address your needs and your new life. For example, you know that reproduction early-American dining room table you picked up from a flea market that doesn't go with anything you have? The one that was okay at the time simply because it had a top? Today, you might want to reassess it, not just in terms of the table itself but also of the

BEFORE

Paint can transform even the most mundane environment of the past into one you can live with in the future.

AFTER

space it takes up. Remember, part of this last purging is taking a fresh, realistic look at your needs. Ask yourself how you really use the piece and the space in question.

- Do I actually eat at the dining room table? Or is it really where I do a lot of my office work and where I sort my mail?

- Do I actually dine in the dining room? Or could this room serve multiple purposes with a round table at one end and an armoire at the other, giving me more usable space?

If you decide you really don't need a dining room table, then you've already agreed to eliminate it altogether. If, however, you still do want a conventional dining room table, can the one in question be reclaimed? Will paint help? Maybe covering the wood with an interesting solid color will distract the eye from its dated style. Now, will you actually do the work? Be honest.

I know it sounds contradictory for me of all people, the "you-can-do-it guy," to suddenly be warning you against do-it-yourself projects, but I am warning you. If you have successfully completed projects for the home and you enjoyed doing them, then knock yourself out. However, if you're simply trying to save money but don't have a track record of completing projects, then chances are slim that you will begin now. I don't want you trapped into false expectations. I do want you to be realistic about what you can do, and more important, what you will do. This is not to say that you can't decorate and make things look nice, but it's my experience that you're either the crafty type or you're not. And if you're not, don't feel guilty about it. Use that energy somewhere else!

How about reevaluating furniture and spatial functions in other areas of the house? "Reclaiming" applies to more than just tchotchkes and chairs; it's about reclaiming space as well.

This take on the old wall bed concept provides a worktable by day and sweet dreams at night.

DUAL FUNCTION GUEST ROOM

If you don't have a place for sleepover guests but wish you did, look beyond the obvious. You may find that a sleeper sofa in the living room fits your needs better than a conventional sofa. Or you may have an alcove suitable for a daybed. When not in use for sleeping, the daybed provides additional seating and is therefore more valuable than a single club chair that takes up almost as much room. (See page 127.)

BOOKCASE BONANZA One small bookcase monopolizing a valuable wall may not be what you need. Consider these alternatives:

- Three bookcases side by side could be very effective in using every inch of wall space to its full potential.

- Two bookcases facing each other against a wall with a hollow-core door between them gives you an instant built-in for work and storage.

- Short bookcases surrounding the back and sides of your sofa create useful storage on three sides. (See page 102.)

A pole, a hollow-core door, and a wardrobe mirror create an instant closet that also promotes good design.

HALLWAYS

You may have a hallway that you've considered only as a pass-through space, but you're in desperate need of storage. With a few overhead shelves or the addition of floor-to-ceiling shelving on one wall, combined with decorative storage containers, you might be home free. (See page 137.)

CLOSETS

You may not have built-in closets ample for your needs. How about creating a closet out of hollow-core doors and a few feet of plumbing pipe? (See pages 144 and 150.)

WORK CENTERS

You might not have space for a freestanding workspace, but by building wall to wall with ready-to-assemble pieces, you might find you even have space to spare. (See page 129.)

I encourage you really to study the room makeovers beginning on page 94 as a way of assessing whether what you currently own is truly serving you in the best way. Read the text as well. There are so many ways to reclaim and update—easily and inexpensively, too!

BEFORE

TURNING THE TABLES You might have mismatched tables throughout your home that hold only one or two things and don't enhance your design. Think about the following options:

- Three suitcases topped with a piece of glass allows you additional surface while providing storage for things you use only now and then, like Christmas decorations.

- If the only reason for a table is to support a lamp, maybe a floor lamp is a better use of the space.

- If all your glass coffee table does is display clutter, then back-to-back storage chests supporting the same glass top might be more effective.

- An ottoman or two and a serving tray will do the same thing as a coffee table, as well as provide extra seating when needed.

BEFORE

GOT PAINT? At this juncture, with everything sort of pulled apart, you may decide you want to paint the walls. This would be a logical time to do it, as your stuff (what's left of it) can simply be moved into the center of your room and covered. In fact, any improvements you might want to make to the shell of your room will be easier to do at this point than after you've got everything pulled together again. For more on color, see Layer One of my first book, *Christopher Lowell's Seven Layers of Design*, or go online to explore how my new Color Courage kit can make this process easier for you.

This plain, underused trunk that was holding up a TV "grew" some legs and turned into a more useful and striking piece of furniture with added storage below and space for display above.

AFTER

BELOW, LEFT AND RIGHT: Van Dyke's Restorers sells this cool spring mechanism as well as great "antique" hardware to turn a simple box into this piece of multifunctioning furniture: a coffee table with storage that turns into a desk.

THE GREAT AWAKENING

Has it hit you yet? A lot of people find themselves halfway into the purging process, only to realize that they're disconnected from far more in their homes than they ever imagined. Experts tell me that this revelation hits hard as people come to understand how much of what they own is suddenly no longer acceptable to them. Ask yourself these questions:

- Am I interested in living with more junk or with more quality?

- Am I holding on to junk because I'm afraid that if it goes I won't have good stuff to replace it?

- Am I holding on to stuff because I don't know what to replace it with?

- Am I not deserving of an upgrade in life?

- Am I afraid my new, clutter-free life might not come with the wisdom and maturity to make better choices?

- Am I really afraid of starting over?

If the answer to any of these questions is yes, you're doing great. It means that you're looking at your life honestly and that it's only your confidence that might be a little rocky right now. Remember, you're breaking bad habits. I know, they were *your* bad habits, dang it! And you had gotten used to them.

It's perfectly natural to have feelings of loss about something even though you know it's no good for you. Sometimes we fear giving up anything, good or bad, because we don't know what we'll replace it with. Or we fear that once we do give up bad habits, we'll disappoint ourselves by backsliding. Banish this fear in favor of trusting that the life ahead will really be better than the one behind you. You're not starting over, you're reinventing.

LAYER 4
SORT
& CONTAIN

At this point, everything you don't want, don't need, and shouldn't have should be gone. Congratulations!

Now that you have made space in closets and drawers and on shelves, you can actually see the stuff that needs to be sorted and contained. In this layer we'll do just that, and we'll figure out what to conceal and what to display, and where to put it all. We'll even make it easy for you with a room-by-room breakdown of some of the most common storage problems and our most brilliant solutions (if I do say so myself). At the end of this chapter we'll discuss the decorative aspects of containing and the containers themselves, which will lead us to Layer Five, Design & Build. So hang on.

For the time being, you probably still have stuff in piles, and that is fine. Your goal now is to sort it into two categories, what will be stored out of sight and what will be stored visibly. If you're undecided about an item, put it in a third "undecided" category for right now. Once you get the hang of the sorting process, these "undecided" items will be easily dealt with. Okay, here we go.

In general, concealed storage is for items you prefer to keep out of view because they're just not pleasant to look at—power tools, toilet paper, giant boxes of Pampers. No matter what the item is, there's a container out there waiting for it, and we've got the Resources to prove it (page 170).

Visible and decorative storage is for the items you don't mind seeing—items that, if contained decoratively, can actually enhance the look and feel of a room, while also fulfilling a function.

How do you decide to hide or not to hide? It might sound basic, but there are some items you may think should be hidden that don't have to be. Towels might be rolled and arranged on open shelves or in baskets, for example. Pastas and cereals can be kept in clear glass canisters on the counter, clearing your precious pantry space.

And guess what? The more you can display, the less you'll have to put away in concealed storage areas—premium real estate, as you'll soon find out.

Train your eye. By using your imagination and looking at the colors and textures of everyday items in a whole new way, you can reserve the precious space in your cupboards, dressers, and closets for only what you don't want visible. The next time you're in an apothecary shop, a clothing boutique, or a gift shop, note how their displays make everything appealing. You can do the same at home.

NEAREST IS DEAREST

Putting things closest to where you use them will make mundane jobs a pleasure. And while it's common sense, many people just don't give themselves the time to think these things through. Do yourself a favor: Every time something isn't where it *logically should be*, move it immediately until everything is in its proper place—as close to where you use it as can be.

Just as in your purging phases, sorting and containing is best done room by room. You will no doubt move things from

room to room depending on your home's configuration. What's important here is that you also sort your concealed storage items by frequency of use.

Meanwhile, sort your concealed storage items into three groups: seldom, occasional, and every day. The idea is to fill the more remote spaces with what you hardly use first, reserving the easiest-to-get-to areas of your home for what you use most frequently.

Seldom

Things like turkey roasters, holiday decorations, winter clothing, vacation gear, legal records, and keepsakes all fall into this category. Stored under beds, on tippy-top shelves, in chests or closed wicker baskets that double as side tables, or in garages and attics, these are things you'll work the hardest to get to. Be clever about your "hiding spots"—you have more than you realize. And don't worry about the hassle of retrieving these things, since you'll have to do so only about once a year.

Occasional

This is stuff you use once in a while but more frequently than once a year. You shouldn't have to work as hard to get to these things as you would the seldom-used item. Some of this stuff will consist of bulk items you'll need access to occasionally, to replenish your daily supplies. These items could include extra staples, Post-it notes, paper clips, Q-tips, cotton balls, and so forth.

Every Day

These are items you use at least three times a week. You don't want them visible, but they have to be handy. It's this stuff that you want to reserve for the most convenient areas of the home. You may have to use your imagination (especially in tight quarters) to actually reserve the choice spots for the stuff you really use every day. Think in terms of gadgets as well as supplies. The TV clicker, the stapler, scissors, pads and pens, dishwashing liquid, and so on.

Just promise me you'll never rummage through occasionally used stuff to get to the stuff you use every day. Period!

Let's start sorting room by room, beginning with the smallest and saving the kitchen for last. Notice that in some cases, I suggest you take certain items normally "belonging" to a certain room and put them somewhere else. It's all about creativity, right?

"Sort your concealed storage items into three groups: seldom, occasional, and every day."

STORING COMMERCIAL PRODUCTS

Many commercial products can be removed from their original packaging and stored or displayed in another, possibly more decorative, container. From dog food to clothespins, if the texture and color of the product are pleasing to the eye, glass containers can be an inexpensive way to display utilitarian commercial products while adding a design element to the room and freeing valuable cupboard and drawer space.

BATHROOMS

Towels of the same color don't have to burden your linen closet. They can be rolled and arranged in large baskets, in odd-size wall nooks, on ledges or shelves, or under a side table. As to where you put them, think about how you use them. If you get out of the shower and towel off first, don't put the towel way over on the towel rack just because it was there when you moved in. Put a basket of towels beside your tub or shower stall. Save the ones on the rack by the sink for drying your hands or reserve them for guests. You can disperse your towels into the various rooms where they are used or where your guests might be using them. Because towels have color and texture, think of them as display items for your master suite, bathrooms, and guest rooms. Think spa . . . think hotel suite.

Toiletries such as hand soaps, moisturizers, and body creams can be transferred into uniform, decorative dispensers now available at most bed and bath shops. As for everyday items such as cotton balls and cosmetics brushes, consider keeping them on the counter in stainless or Plexiglas containers that are both pretty and functional.

The rest of what's left after the big purge is not necessarily what you'll need or use every day. For example, if you regularly blow-dry your hair, but use hot rollers only when you really dress up, keep the dryer in a basket near the vanity, or hang it on a nail near where you use it. Park the rollers and other seldom-used products in a well-marked container in the linen closet or under the sink, not next to your deodorant. If you give yourself a mud mask or a hot-oil hair treatment just once a month, don't store these products next to the perfume you use daily. You get the idea, right?

"Because towels have color and texture, think of them as display items..."

CLOTHES CLOSETS

When it comes to sweaters and folded clothing, think about walking into a boutique designed so that the eye goes to the color of the clothing. You can do the same at home. Stacks of brightly colored sweaters neatly folded can look great displayed on a closet shelf, but how about in a bedroom bookcase? Why not? Then your closets get freed up for things that need to be hung and remain wrinkle free.

As for the rest of it, unless you're a showgirl, how often will you be sporting the gold lamé, rhinestone-encrusted clutch with the tiara and shoes that match? I have twelve pairs of cuff links but spend most of my time in pullovers—dig? Store your special-event clothing somewhere else besides your everyday closet. Special-occasion clothes and accessories can be stored in stackable, covered containers that live out of sight in myriad places other than the everyday closet.

You'll most likely have these glam clothes freshly dry-cleaned before you wear them anyway, so don't worry that they are packed away. Enough said.

BEDROOMS AND LIVING ROOMS

I'll deal with these rooms briefly now since they are more about design (Layer Five) than sorting and containing. They do, however, benefit from good organization as much as any other room does. Because they are where you either rest or spend quality time with your family and friends, these rooms should be especially clutter free and therefore distraction free. Here are some organization ideas to get you thinking.

If you use the extra blanket in the chest at the foot of your bed only now and then but have no place to put the throw pillows that come off your bed nightly, put the blanket in the linen closet and reserve the chest for your throw pillows.

If you find yourself getting out of bed or out of the chair thirty times a night to get the TV guide, the aspirin, the note cards, the body moisturizer, the bottled water, and the clicker, put them all in one organized basket and place it next to you, on the bed or by the chair or wherever.

OFFICE AREAS

There are entire books devoted to the organization of offices and files and so forth, so I am focusing here on clutter control and making it look good. I am such a fanatic about this that I designed an entire line of office furniture and accessories for Office Depot, so you may want to give it a look, for inspiration if nothing more!

Meanwhile, keep handy the items you use regularly and sort them in nifty drawer dividers or containers on your desk.

But what about the extras? Say you had special "From the desk of" cards printed. Usually you need to order at least a hundred to get a price break. Keep a few in a drawer close by and store the rest in a closed decorative container on the top shelf of your office workstation.

For reference materials, pamphlets, periodicals, manuals, et cetera, that you need occasionally but don't like the looks of, magazine holders can get the job done. They load from the back, but when displayed on a shelf side by side, their uniform spines can be labeled for easy identification without exposing all the mismatched items inside.

UTILITY ROOMS AND CLOSETS

Small hand tools, flashlights, extension cords, picture hangers, lightbulbs, candles, sewing kits, shoe shine supplies, and so on are all things you probably don't use every day, but you want to find them when you need them. (And it drives you crazy when you can't.) These can be stored in uniform decorative baskets so that when you do need these handy items, you can take the whole basket where you need it and then return it when you're done. This makes a lot more sense than having a junk drawer filled with things you thought were there but can never find because they're hidden in the back of the drawer.

KITCHENS AND DINING AREAS

Everybody needs to eat, so here more than anywhere, you must take a hard look at what you use every day and what you use occasionally.

Appliances and specialty cookware are the biggest space-robbing culprits. Things like fish poachers, waffle irons, the big food processor (versus the little one you use nightly), the Bundt pan, the bread maker, the ice-cream maker, even the espresso machine, get far less use than we might care to admit. The double boiler and the food mill are good to have when a recipe dictates, but not every day. While the salad spinner is a nice touch when company comes over, most of us buy a bag of prewashed greens to use on a nightly basis. If the deep fryer only gets used once a month (if that), tuck it back

"In kitchens, organization is key."

into a hard-to-reach spot or get it out of the kitchen altogether. This will leave the easy-to-reach areas free for everyday preparation. It's okay to have a fish poacher under the guest bed if that's the only place you have room for it. Who's to know?

For your everyday pots, pans, and utensils, consider overhead racks, metal grids, or Peg-Boards, all within your easy reach.

If you use a variety of olive oils when you cook everyday meals, don't put them in the pantry. Place them on a decorative tray and display them on the counter where you can grab them. If you season most of your food next to your stovetop, don't put the spice drawer next to your dishwasher where the silverware should go (for easy unloading).

As for food items, cereals, pastas, grains, and beans can look wonderful lining your counters in uniform glass containers. Fruits and vegetables that don't require refrigeration and are consumed in a timely fashion can be placed in bowls and baskets all around the house. In my living room, which opens to my dining room, I have everything from lemons and limes to red onions and potatoes heaped in containers looking very bountiful.

Like clothing, bright-colored linens, napkins, and place mats can look great folded neatly in open shelves, leaving drawers free for kitchen gadgets you don't want to see. Now, if you only use tablecloths on the rare occasions when you entertain, don't put them in the same drawer or on the same shelf as the place mats you use every day. Put the fancy tablecloths where you'll occasionally get to them and put the place mats as close to the table as possible.

Look for great storage ideas
in this open kitchen.

A sideboard stacked with various-size dinner plates and serving pieces can create a great vignette while adding a very "bistro" attitude to a dining area or kitchen.

ATTENTION, "BULK" SHOPPERS! With warehouse club shopping so popular today, many people find that they save money but don't know where to put the bulk. Large containers that can be labeled and stacked work best for these items. Toilet paper, paper towels, canned soda, and bottled water come under this category. And for those of you who have attics, utility rooms, and garages (which by now should be almost empty, right?), that's where this stuff goes. For those of you who don't have areas outside your immediate living space, find someone to split the bulk with so you both get the savings but not the storage problem. The same goes with bulk office supplies. Find someone to share a carton of printer paper, pads, and boxes of pens with so you get the value without the bulk.

In my guest house, I have my towels and sheets dispersed among all the bedrooms. This frees up what was once my linen closet, which is now used for all my bulk storage. Get it?

PROGRESS REPORT, REALITY CHECK, AND LET THE FUN BEGIN!

By now, the hardest places to get to should be designated and maybe even already filled with your least-used items. Some of your concealed occasional storage should also be dealt with without having to encroach on the prime real estate reserved for your concealed everyday stuff.

What you have left over, plus your "visible" storage and decorative items, will help you determine the kinds of containers and furniture you'll need to purchase going forward.

At this stage you're ready to embrace what's left in your home—the things that still have meaning to you and that promote productivity. At any rate what's left should be only the furniture and objects that tell your story accurately. If you are still on the fence about a few items, that's okay. You've got three more layers to go. Remember, you're starting to go through a change that brings with it new decisions, new priorities, and new vision. It's all a part of the exciting adventure we call reinvention!

This is a good time to give yourself a break and take a walk through places like Hold Everything, Cost Plus, Pier 1, IKEA, Office Depot, Burlington Coat Factory, Target, and the like. Many of these stores have Web sites that will allow you to browse from home. Look to see exactly what will serve your containing needs *and* look good in your home—because the next phase is Layer Five: Design & Build.

It's where the real fun starts.

> "What's left should be only the furniture and objects that tell your story accurately."

BIN THERE, DONE THAT

Let's get into the container discussion. Decorative containers these days come in a variety of shapes, sizes, and colors. When using them in mass, remember that whatever material you choose, be it wicker, tin, bamboo, or enamel, will become a significant design element. Below are a few of my notes and preferences.

Shape

Round containers with lids are better when stacked on surfaces like tabletops and desks. Deep baskets can be used on the floor to store tall rolls of wrapping paper, rolled towels, and the like. Placing houseplants and trees into deep round floor containers will help further integrate the texture you've chosen for your storage containers below eye level.

For shelves, I like square or rectangle containers versus round. Round containers take up too much space and don't fit well side by side.

Covered or Open

If I'm using bins on shelves, I prefer them uncovered from eye level up. They're easier to get into and out of. However, for seldom-used concealed storage items, which may be placed on high shelves or stacked on the floor, lids allow you to stack them in graduated sizes for a great look.

Metal and Enamel

Many of these bins do not come with lids but are sturdy and will take a lot of abuse. Enamel does have a tendency to chip, so keep that in mind. While many come with handles, many do not come with a place to put a label so you know what's inside. For labeling, I love using inexpensive luggage tags, which you can get at travel stores and luggage shops.

See-Through Containers

What can I say? I find them limiting when used in decorated rooms. On the other hand, as useful containers in closets, under beds, or in attics or basements, they're the best, and far sturdier and safer for long-term storage than cardboard boxes. Here again, do yourself a favor and look for crates and containers that have lids. These allow you to stack efficiently to maximize space.

Containers with Linings

Many wicker bins and baskets are available with cloth liners. These are ideal for bedrooms, where socks and lingerie can be stashed and will be safe from snagging. They will also free up dresser drawers. They tend to be visually more at home in laundry areas, bedrooms, and bathrooms but may be a bit fussy and less streamlined for your public spaces such as living and dining rooms.

Some of these linings are piped with floral or geometric patterns. Steer clear of these, as they will lock pattern into something you might want to remain more versatile.

Utility Areas

Just because you don't linger in these spaces doesn't mean you should hate being in them. Treat your garages, attics, and mudrooms with dignity, as they are vital, hardworking areas of the home. They can also be fun to superorganize top to bottom.

Canisters for Concealed Storage

To be sure, there are items (usually commercial products, office supplies, toiletries, and food-related stuff) that you use all the time. Instead of finding the package, opening it, getting what you need, closing the package, and reshelving it, you might want to pop a container lid off and on instead. I know, duh! But it's something we do all the time without even thinking about it.

Finding solid canisters that are attractive and unadorned is tricky. I found square black pottery canisters with stainless-steel tops, which I have lined up in my home office. They store everything from binder clips and rubber bands to ink cartridges and pens—none of which is attractive enough to place in clear containers. But I didn't find these canisters at an office-supply store, I found them in the kitchen section of a (primarily) bath and linen shop. They were designed to hold coffee—hello! The point is, use your imagination. If it's got a lid and holds stuff, it's a canister, baby!

Canisters for Visible Storage

Clear canisters are easier to come by and add a great apothecary look to bathrooms and kitchens. I bought two dozen eight-inch jars with glass lids at a restaurant-supply store for $6 apiece and placed them on floor-to-ceiling shelves I installed on a small wall in my bathroom. I filled the glass jars with everything from potpourri and bars of soap to candles, Q-tips, makeup sponges, clothespins, and even rolls of toilet paper. When it was all finished it looked amazing. I liked it so much that I repeated the same thing in my kitchen, where they held enough stuff to let me empty out six of my kitchen drawers, leaving them for stuff I didn't want visible.

This proves the point that there is power in mass. Three jars would have looked simply utilitarian, but twenty-four made a design statement and were practical to boot! Love that!

READY, SET, SHOP!

With your design notes and a tight shopping list, it's time to get out there and find the stuff that has your name on it. Once you get it all home, move storage units and containers around until you have them where you want them *before* you fill them.

While you're shopping, if you're not sure about an item, don't buy it, or make sure you can return it. Don't put pressure on yourself to make critical decisions until you're comfortable. Take your time. Focus on one area of your home at a time. If you have to make several trips to the same place, so be it. A happy shopper makes a happy decorator.

MORE PURGING, ANYONE?

As you bring home new goods to contain all your stuff, you'll have another chance to look at everything before you load in the effects of your new life. If at any point you stop and wonder why you kept something, it probably means you shouldn't have. You've come a long way, baby, and you're changing every second. Your ideas about who you are and how you'll live are evolving swiftly. Reserve the right to change your mind. A changing mind is a mind that's making changes. And you will continue to eliminate more things from your life as you become clearer about what you really need.

You're making discerning choices. You're beginning to take a vital interest in how you live and what you live with. This is excellent. With luck, the fascination and curiosity about the way you live will become second nature for the rest of your life.

KEEP IT SIMPLE When shopping for storage units and containers, keep the motif simple. Avoid little doodads and painted designs, which will lock pattern into the long-term investments you're about to make. Think in terms of texture and solid elements that will work wherever you put them.

Storage units such as bookcases and shelves should be simple and unadorned as a background for what you'll put in them. Let your decorative accessories and your textured containers do all the work. A potted plant here and a little figurine there will showcase much better against a neutral surface than against a purple laminated bookcase with little brass tacks you thought would go with your bedspread. You'll pay for all these extras when in fact you don't need them. By the time they're filled with all the things you love, how much of the surface will you really see?

LAYER 5
DESIGN
& BUILD

To embark on Layer Five, your home, for the most part, should be clutter free … a bit pulled apart but with newfound space. Your sorting process should be nearly finished, and you should have a pretty good idea about where stuff will go. You should also have begun to make your list of things you'll need to purchase for the rest of your storage needs.

Throughout this essentially solitary experience you've no doubt been thinking about all sorts of things. I'm sure your mind has wandered in many directions as you have plucked up the courage to make important decisions about the life you're leaving behind for the new way of life you are creating. And by now you are well out of your comfort zone, right?

When you take physical action to make change, everything changes. It's a chain reaction that, fostered by honest self-examination, brings a whole new set of creative considerations. You are no doubt beginning to suspect that the fear that prevented you from changing has been more detrimental than the changes themselves. This is what I mean when I say where there is fear, there is no creativity. Still, it takes guts and faith to step into the world of the unknown, even when it's your own closets and cupboards.

And now you know. The physical junk you were getting rid of is directly connected to the mental junk you've been carrying around in your head for so long. You're freeing space in your mind—space in which to think creatively.

Now let's get down to the nitty-gritty. The Design & Build layer breaks down into three phases.

PHASE 1: THINK IT THROUGH

"What's this room's story?" Is it about multitasking? Two people sharing the same room who need to work and relax in the same space? Whatever your new story is, write it down. You want the "new" space to reflect who you are *now* and who you want to become. List everything you want the room to do for you. Don't rush this process. Think of it as though you and your new home-to-be are dating. You want to get to know everything about it before making the commitment to live with it in a whole new way.

BUDGING THE BUDGET
You're investing in your new life!

With the worldwide sources available to retailers today, a lot of containers and storage units may be less expensive now than they were the last time you looked. In fact, many of these products didn't even exist until recently. Nevertheless, this is where you'll have to start spending a buck or two, and it's worth it to keep you from slipping back into bad habits.

While I don't advocate going into debt, I do advocate that you review what you have spent your money on historically. When we're not feeling good about our lives, we tend to spend more money than we realize in an attempt to escape boredom.

When you put your expenditures into new perspective, you may find that there's more money available to you than you thought. In fact, it's why there's such a huge boom in the home improvement market. People are reprioritizing. Instead of spending on vacations to escape their lives at home, they're investing *to enjoy* their lives at home.

PHASE 2: DESIGN

What do you need to add to the room to achieve your goal, and what's already there that you can play off of? Is the window high enough from the floor to place a workstation under it? Could you add overhead shelves?

To configure the space, use masking tape on the floor to outline furniture to see how much space will be used, estimating for those pieces you haven't yet acquired. Even we pros are surprised at how much can go in a small space. Consider the aesthetics as well. Will a fresh coat of paint and an updated window treatment enhance your productivity here? If it makes you happier to be there, the answer is yes.

PHASE 3: BUILD

Establish a timeline for your progress. If you find that creating the environment you want will take more time or money than you thought, consider painting the space and leaving it at that for a while. A rich new wall color is the cheapest way to transform a space and will get your creative juices flowing. If we tackle painting and built-ins first, we may realize that the room needs far less furniture than we previously thought. Work in stages, if your time and budget dictate, and work from the outside in, as I discuss in *Seven Layers of Design*, with the "accessories," including your storage containers, which we're coming to, I promise.

From here on, I'd like you to flip through the rest of the book periodically for creative inspiration as you consider ways to maximize your home in a whole new way. If you read carefully, you'll realize that we've used only inexpensive materials from neighborhood stores. And to get you to think outside the box, we've used a lot of the same things repeatedly, in a variety of ways. Our goal is to help you to look at conventional things in an unconventional way. Note how we've positioned simple things like bookcases to do far more than hold books. In doing so we've also created more storage than we'll ever need (well, maybe). And of course, the very best part is that you won't need a carpenter or workshop to do what we've done.

SPACE: THE FINAL FRONTIER

Start with a clean slate. Forget about how you've positioned your furniture in the past. By not reverting to old ideas of how you lived in your last life, you can make fresh considerations for your new one. It may be the same space, but you're no longer in the same place mentally, so don't be afraid to seek new options, no matter how crazy or unconventional they are. It's your house, not your mother's or your sister's.

WHAT TO BUY

Because you'll shop at the same stores as we do, and because we too offer merchandise at retail stores nationwide, learn from us. Most of what you will find in the marketplace comes in what is deemed best-selling colors.

As to the items themselves, look for sturdy construction, flexibility, and quality you can live with. It is better to have a few things of good quality than a lot of shabby stuff (that in the long run you won't be happy with). You might need ten wicker containers but can only afford five. Stick with the five and get more as you can afford them, especially if the containers will be where you can see them. Remember that, besides storing your things, the containers' function is to look great as a design element in your new home.

The same goes for any furniture you might purchase. On a limited budget, an excellent option is ready-to-assemble furniture. Nothing wrong with that. Be aware, however, that it comes in varying levels of quality. Just because you put it together yourself at home doesn't mean it has to look like you did.

Keep in mind that retailers sometimes make their own deals with manufacturers, and it's all about volume. The more they can sell, the better your deal will be. That's why you will usually find lower prices at chain stores than at small local specialty shops. So don't price a bookcase thinking that they'll all be that same price. The more you shop and compare, the more you'll save.

Try mail-order catalogues as well. By cutting out the middleman and going direct, you can often save more to get better quality.

CHOOSING YOUR BOOKCASES

Bookcases with legs work well as stand-alone pieces. They give the appearance of self-contained furniture. These are pieces you'll use on a wall as a focal point with other furniture or art. If you need several cases side by side, however, you're best to buy them with a solid "kick plate," or board spanning the space between the bottom shelf and the floor. These give a clean, continuous surface along the bottom and have a more built-in look.

If you want the ability to configure your bookcases in different ways, it is best if the case is flush to the floor. Then the cases can be stacked, placed back-to-back in the center of a room, or placed perpendicular to the wall. (See page 38.)

BEFORE

AFTER

A WORD ON ASSEMBLY If you're not as handy or as patient as you'd care to admit, or you don't have the right tools, you might want to consider having a professional do the delivery and assembly for you. For a nominal fee, places like Office Depot will bring the item (no matter how big) to your door, unpack it, assemble it, and remove the trash. If you can afford it, do it! If you know you'll be building, say, a wall of bookcases to divide a space, make sure you have wood screws available so that you or your professional installer can bolt them together for safety and strength.

> "Your mental interior matches your home's interior. When one changes, the other changes, too."

THROUGH THICK AND THIN

The thickness of the wood on a bookshelf does make a difference. The thicker the shelf, the more modern and substantive it looks. On page 101 we've used a Lack unit from IKEA, which has thick walls and sides for a very sleek, modern look that can integrate into almost any room. However, on page 129 we've built a combined storage and worktable using simple cases with much thinner sides and shelves. You decide which you prefer. In other makeovers we added our own trim around shelves and cases for a similar look for less money.

Most ready-to-assemble bookcases and hutches come with very thin backs. These backs are surprisingly sturdy when nailed all the way around, but they often do not match the rest of the unit. If that is the case, the backboard can be painted an accent color, or if you want it to appear more open, paint the inside of the back the same color as the walls. Affixed mirror tiles can also reflect the rest of the space and can be secured with Mirror Mastic or with the rubber adhesive pads that come with the tiles.

For shelving units that have no backs, wardrobe mirrors, Peg-Board, or fabric panels can be added if you choose to place the units where the backs might be in view. And don't forget you can also place units back-to-back.

ADJUSTABLE OR NOT?

As far as I'm concerned, the more versatile the piece, the better. This goes for adjustable shelves, too. In ready-to-assemble pieces, I like both. A few nonadjustable shelves make the unit stronger. When storing uniform containers in bookshelves, keep in mind that the adjustable feature is a must. The closer the next shelf is to the top of your container, the less you can see it.

KEEP A WISH BOOK Build a scrapbook, start a three-ring binder, or make a set of files to keep track of magazine pictures and photos of your wish-list items. It's also great to share these photos with others as you enroll them into the world of your possibilities. With more eyes out there looking, you're more apt to find what you want.

A GLASS ACT

You can always take a shelf from your bookcase to a glass shop and have them cut a shelf for you using the wooden shelf as the template. Suddenly a ho-hum bookcase is transformed into a great-looking curio cabinet. With the addition of lighting, which we'll talk about in the next layer—oh, my gosh—total upgrade. And no one will ever suspect!

HARDWARE UPGRADES

Sometimes ready-to-assemble furniture comes with wimpy knobs (which keep the price down). Don't be afraid to upgrade the hardware for a great designer look at a fraction of the cost. This is a good way to dress up existing furniture, too!

DOORS OR NOT

Some units give you the option of adding doors for concealed storage—from counter height down to the floor. I strongly recommend this. Lower doors take up much less visual space than overhead doors do and offer more storage flexibility.

ON MIXING WOODS Most of what will be available to you in ready-to-assemble furniture is what's called "photo-laminate." It's basically a photograph of real wood, laminated over particleboard. With today's digital photography, these laminates are better than ever and really do look genuine. Having said that, don't try to match the wood to whatever you might already own, because it never will. Comparing real wood to laminate does both an injustice. The rule of thumb here is to go at least three shades lighter or darker so it's obvious that you're not trying for a dead-on match. Keep in mind that the wood (or laminate) is only a background. The versatility will be in how you display it—but that's the next layer.

ARRANGE
& DISPLAY

Let the real fun begin!

The art of display is purely about what pleases your eye. If you think it looks cool, then it does! I will warn you, however, that this layer is never really finished. I have built-in bookshelves on both sides of my fireplace filled with pottery, majolica, and porcelain that I've been collecting for years. At least once a week I find myself up on a stool moving things around—playing, really. I can't help it. I'll be talking on the phone, look up, and suddenly wonder if the plate on the top shelf would look better in back of the small figure on the third shelf. And, well ... off I go. Every time someone comes over the shelves look completely different.

Showcasing your items is magical because everything the human hand deliberately touches has a way of smiling back at you. In *Seven Layers of Design*, I devote an entire chapter to this topic. But in this book we'll just cover some of the basics. Here again, the room photos illustrate these principles in case reading about them doesn't cut it for you, okay?

REMEMBER, YOU ARE CREATIVE!

If you can get dressed, style your hair, and drive a car in busy traffic, you are not only creative but also more than quali-fied to make decorating decisions in the home. You may not be a talented genius, but you are, by virtue of being human, creative. But that creativity gets trampled on when self-esteem is low and fear is ruling. So banish the thought that you cannot make your home look pleasing.

Let's start with . . .

ARRANGING

This is simply putting things in a logical order. You've got six baskets and six shelves. What do you do? Put three baskets each on two shelves. How bad is that? Okay, that's one look, but how about one basket in the center of six shelves, creat-ing a graphic stripe down the entire bookcase, and then fill-ing both sides with books?

See, you can do whatever pleases your eye, and the more options you try, the more fun you'll have (or the more nuts it will make you).

Arranging is also about neatness and uniformity. A stack of towels or sweaters folded every which way won't be nearly as effective as the stack folded uniformly. If you fill a large glass container with random, unrelated items, it won't make nearly the same impact as if you fill the container with all of one thing.

Arrangement and organization work hand in hand to cre-ate a deliberate order. When working with multiples of the same things like baskets or canisters, the simpler, the better. You'll find that the grouping itself *is* the design. There is power in numbers.

Before beginning the actual arranging, however, first place your things in the general area where you think they belong. This will give you an at-a-glance idea of what you have and the space you've allocated for it. You'll have a chance to tweak it later; we'll cover that, too.

Now for the next step.

BOTTOM LOAD

VERTICAL STRIPE

STAGGERED

DIAGONAL

DISPLAY

Some of the best clues come from the retail business, where the art of display is referred to as *merchandising*. In fact, the best way to get ideas is by actually going to your favorite store and observing how the store's organization and décor make you love and want everything! Good merchandising is simply good storytelling. And now that you (I hope) have kept only the stuff that tells your story, this should be a breeze.

Call it what you want: futzing, fluffing, finessing. It's all the same thing—merchandising. And what every designer knows is that a finished room is in the details. Good merchandising can mix the mundane with the special and make everything look like a million bucks. It has little to do with money and all to do with your playful, creative spirit. And while this effort is decidedly more, dare I say, artistic than mere "arranging," there is no wrong way to do it as long as it pleases you. And yet there are principles of arranging and merchandising that many of the pros follow. Let's do a quick overview, shall we?

POWER BY NUMBERS

Clustering like items together gives them an importance and design panache they wouldn't have on their own.

The twelve pewter spoons you've collected and placed here and there may look like clutter or as if you had a soup party but forgot to clean up. Take those same twelve spoons, mount them in a shadow box, and hang it on the wall. Then you've made a statement: "I collect spoons, and here they are looking really special."

A tin bucket sitting by itself on a table looks like someone forgot it on the way to the woodshed. But six buckets filled with seashells and lined up on a weathered sideboard is simple and stunning. Get it? It's power in numbers that tells a story about you: "I'm creative, and I love the beach."

Twenty vintage postcards tucked here and there or piled in a bowl look like an afterthought. Filling a wall with them all framed identically is a major statement. See how one simple thing can be showcased to become a room's focal point?

Identical bins scattered between four or five bookcases throughout a room lose their impact. But an entire bookcase of identical bins can provide floor-to-ceiling texture, depending on what your bins are made of.

"Good merchandising displays a room in its best light by telling all who enter that you thought about what goes where."

I collect men's leather hatboxes, which I have in my beach house master suite stacked on an armoire and arranged in clusters on various glass tables around the room. The hatboxes are home to loose change, jewelry, travel items such as passports and currency converters, and maps of places I visit frequently. Everything is stored according to use. The filled hatboxes free up my dresser while adding a rich haberdashery feeling to the space.

ABOVE Mars versus Venus: His trophies and her teacups *can* live together.

LEFT Clustering like items together gives them importance

POWER BY COLOR

Color is the great unifier. It can make unrelated objects relate, so it's an easy and inexpensive way to create a great still life. It's also a nifty way to organize a collection.

I have been collecting chartreuse-colored pottery for years (ahem, long before it was in vogue, thank you). Rather than scatter pieces throughout the house like Easter eggs, I put the

"The art of placement adds a sense of order to an ordinary set of shelves, becoming part of the design."

collection all in the same room for maximum drama. I've received many compliments on my pottery, and friends send me fabulous chartreuse pieces from all over the country because it is obvious I collect them. The point here is that a lot of mismatched stuff, when grouped by the same color, takes on a power of its own and becomes visually striking.

Another favorite little vignette of mine, and a fine example of monochromatic scheming, is an old ironstone bowl (white) propped against a whitewashed architectural element, and a white orchid plant. It's simple, pleasing to the eye, and soothing to the soul because someone cared enough to make it happen.

Think about the objects around your house that may not "go together" but that might be put together in color groups. Experiment. I bet you'll surprise yourself with the creative arrangements you come up with.

The eye goes to color. Adding a fresh new accent color to a room can really give it a pick-me-up. If you add color in curtains, pillows, table skirts, runners, and accessories, you can tie together even the most mismatched furniture.

Once you've decided on a color, use it evenly around the room for visual balance. Try it in a variety of ways, from art on the wall to accessories in your bookshelves, even to the color of your candles. An accent color can really add punch.

If you're feeling insecure about mixing and matching pattern and color, just pick one solid color and call it a day. Bright yellow pillows, sunny artwork, rich wall color, and crisp new curtains will do wonders for the room and for your spirit, too. Go for it!

LIFTS AND LEVELS

A potluck at Aunt Marge's looks like this: several covered dishes lined up on a table. A buffet at the Four Seasons hotel presents food on elevations with cool stuff tucked here and there. The former is about eating; the latter is an event!

The same principle of lifts and levels translates directly to your home in your arrangements of objects, art, and mementos. Plate racks, cubes, pedestals, and anything that gives "lift" to an arrangement—dare I say it—elevates its creativity. (Ooh, bad, I know.)

An antique teacup atop a small stack of books, next to another teacup atop a color-coordinated trinket box, next to another teacup set on the table says "special" in a way that setting them down together at the same height won't.

Lifts and levels, which you can devise with anything that works, is an indispensable tool of display for the things you love.

GROUPING BY THEME

What are your stories? Why do you have what you have? How can you "make it smile" and tell the story of how you are connected to it?

Here's an example: a vintage shoe, a propped-up vintage purse, and on a wire stand (for height) behind them an old postcard from Paris—a fashion shot from the early 1900s. It tells a story.

Certain things just go together:

- A sewing spool, a miniature dress form, and a weaving shuttle

- A ship's model, a bowl of shells, and brass anchor book-ends propping up volumes of seafaring tales

- A lava lamp, a glass bud vase holding a single gerbera daisy, and a pair of fuzzy dice resting on a book about the Rat Pack

Each group of items tells a story. Each might convey what you're interested in and give clues about your personality. Each might spark conversation for you and for others. These

BEFORE

things become mini-shrines, in a sense, devoted to what you're into and what you think is cool. They're reminding you and telling others why you care about what you own.

But don't get carried away. You may get into this still life/ storytelling thing so much that before you know it you've turned the top of a dresser into a Rose Bowl Parade float. That's okay. You got into it and you had fun doing it. So don't tear it all down. Edit it. There isn't an author (me included) who doesn't need editing. There's not an actor who doesn't need directing or a musician who doesn't need conducting. A sophisticated eye comes with practice. Study what you do. Strive to display the objects that tell the simplest story in the most straightforward way, and eliminate the rest.

My team always accuses me of overpropping. I put in all the ideas, and then we edit them down to a few basic things, which tell the story, but in a simpler way. This brings me to another point.

AFTER

Strive to display the objects that tell the simplest story in the
most straightforward way, and eliminate the rest.

Adding four drapery panels to an ordinary bed lends height and drama to the space for little money.

BEFORE

LETTING YOUR ROOM BREATHE

Don't feel you need to fill every nook and cranny. Not every surface needs something on it, and not every inch of wall space needs to be decorated. Allow a bit of empty space where all you might see is an expanse of luscious wall color. How about a tabletop with only one dramatic object on it? Or an alcove with nothing in it but a great view out the window?

Filling empty space just for the sake of it is what got you in trouble in the first place. The art of restraint is just as important in display as it is in arranging. Don't put stuff out simply because you have it. I'd enjoy a sparely but deliberately decorated room far more than one crammed to the rafters—I get a headache just trying to take it all in.

The good news here is that you really don't need a lot to furnish a room. Less is always more when it's well thought out. Take baby steps at first. Play and have fun as you begin to exercise your inherently creative muscles.

AFTER

BEFORE

We attached chenille drapes to half-round shelves, which we lit from the inside to emphasize the height of the windows and create a cozy nook.

AFTER

THE IMPORTANCE OF SCALE

What gives a room presence is height and scale. Designers know that a few large-scale things give a room drama and dynamics, no matter how small the room. When in doubt, go bigger and taller.

Studies (and common sense) tell us we need 18 to 20 inches of space to comfortably get in and around furniture. With that in mind, don't be afraid to increase the size of coffee tables and upholstered pieces in a small room. Small things in a small room can actually make the room look smaller! Here again, try marking furniture outlines on the floor with masking tape to give you a sense of what will actually fit in the room.

For more ideas on dealing with small spaces, you might want to look at *Christopher Lowell's You Can Do It! Small Spaces: Decorating to Make Every Inch Count.*

FURNITURE PLACEMENT

You will create more seating, especially in smaller spaces, by placing sofas and chairs in conversation groups in the center of the room. A large coffee table will anchor the setting while also providing a place to set your drink, the popcorn bowl, current magazines, and so on. Use an area rug to visually define the seating area.

Getting things like sofas away from the walls frees the wall space to accommodate your art and your storage furniture like bookcases and hutches.

RIGHT These stick-on track lights can make even task lighting dramatic as well as create an instant gallery in an underused corner.

"Create an
instant gallery
in an alcove."

CREATING ROOMS WITHIN ROOMS

The photos that follow will give you great ideas for breaking up rooms into more intimate and useful spaces. Bookcases placed perpendicular to walls create a visual passageway to distinguish one area from another. Interrupted space is often more intriguing than an open expanse, which can seem undefined and uninviting. Sometimes thinking outside the box means redefining the box itself.

IT'S ALL IN THE MOOD

Don't forget about lighting. It's the final layer of *Seven Layers of Design*—and the most overlooked. It's easy to set a great mood with the inexpensive lighting available in the marketplace today. (There's even a peel-and-stick track lighting kit that doesn't require an electrician.)

The rule of thumb is that there should be as much shadow as light. It's shadow that gives a room character and intimacy. From picture lights, to cabinet lighting, to up lights and candles, all lighting works together to give a room atmosphere.

Now, do me a favor. Once they're installed, don't save the pretty lights for company. Turn them on at night just for you. You deserve it after all this work. Learn to celebrate your home every day!

PEP TALK

Reading this book and actually making the commitment to change your life are two different things. You must believe that you have the power to handle the process of purging. Don't be afraid of change.

Your new life is waiting for you to claim it. The first step in doing so is to unload your excess baggage (clutter!) so you can travel farther and enjoy the trip. Isn't it time you take the leap of faith? Go ahead, make my day!

Now, enjoy the rest of the book, knowing I'm with you all the way.

LAYER 7
CEASE
& MAINTAIN

Your purging process, like anything you ultimately commit to, must become a way of life. For the moment, everything looks great and you have a sense of renewed spirit. Good for you. But remember, there will always be flea markets, sales, unread magazines, and well-wishers bearing gifts. There will still be junk mail, things that fall apart, things you can live without, and things you just can't. The world of stuff will keep spinning, and moments of weakness will pop up when you least expect them.

Remind yourself of what you've just been through. You're now lean and mean and proud of it. So how do you stay that way? How do you prevent backsliding? By developing a distaste for clutter.

Train yourself to be uncomfortable if everything is not in its place. Make a habit of purging on a continual basis. Don't wait till the end of each month. Things can get mighty out of control in thirty days, believe me. You may feel like a stranger in your own home as you slowly grow into your new life. It's only natural. You'll also feel slightly obsessive about your new digs until you make the daily purging process a habit.

"Let's explore ways to help you stay clutter free."

Once purging becomes second nature, you won't think twice about picking up after yourself. Staying streamlined can become compulsive—to the point that you can't wait to finish the newspaper just so you can throw it away!

People tell us that many reformed junksters even start preaching the virtues of clutter-free living as though it's a newfound religion, because the life change has been so profound for them. Go ahead and share the feeling; it'll cut down on my workload!

Let's explore ways to help you stay clutter free:

- Assign yourself a small "to read" basket. Try to empty it completely by the end of each week. It will give you a good idea of how much time you really have to read, and it may even cause you to cancel a subscription or two. There are magazine racks in every supermarket, and you can flip through the magazines first to see if you really want them—who knew? And there's always the Internet, remember.

- Buy a scanner. They are easy to use and can cut your printed clutter in half. One disk can hold up to a hundred pages. Heck, an entire library could fit in a suitcase.

- Get rid of any computer components you don't use and look for machines that offer more than one function. And, by the way, if you don't ever read those computer manuals, get rid of them.

- Put decorative wastebaskets in every room. Position them next to where you read, by a favorite chair, even under the dining room table until you get in the habit of using them. Empty them often. Don't wait until they are brimming over. (In fact, during these first few weeks, get in the habit of taking out a filled trash bag or two every time you leave the house!)

- Clean out your car and have it washed once a week. I know this seems unrelated to the home, but it's not. It is a reminder away from home that you're in the streamlined mode.

- As you use your bins and baskets, keep looking for things to purge—things you thought you'd use but really don't.

- Toss junk mail before you sit down to read your personal mail. In fact, stand over the trash can while you do it. If you didn't ask for it, chances are you don't need it.

- Don't take something just because it's free or buy something just because it's on sale. And the term "must-have" should be dropped altogether from your vocabulary.

- Don't shop to fill space in your home. Buy only what you need. Make a list and stick to it.

- Learn the difference between upgrading and augmenting. Augmenting is rarely acceptable in your new life because it means "in addition to" instead of "replacing." Whereas to upgrade means to replace a less desirable item for a better one.

- File your bills the moment you receive them. Once they are paid, file the receipts as you seal the outgoing envelopes. Better yet, pay your bills online! One online company, Paytrust (paytrust.com), will even send all your billers change-of-address forms so the bills go directly to them. If for some reason you want a paper copy, you can either print it or request the actual copy by mail. At the end of the year you get a CD-ROM of all your transactions, sorted by categories you set up yourself. It's amazing the amount of time and trouble this saves!

- Purge your wardrobe as you go. If you just tried on a shirt and it doesn't fit or is damaged, get rid of it, don't just hang it back up. Remember the trash bag rule—once an item goes in, it doesn't come out.

- Do your laundry in mini-loads every day. Start a load before you go to work or before bedtime. When it's done, fold the items and put them away, right away. This keeps you from spending a lot of time folding a

lot of clothes in one go, and if you have only a few articles in the laundry at once, it can even cut down on the number of clothes you really need.

- Empty the dishwasher when the cycle is done. If you don't, dirty dishes will pile up in the sink because you can't put them in the dishwasher right away.

- Never leave a room messy. Don't walk out until everything is back where it belongs. And the excuse that you'll be using what's out of place tomorrow is a big no-no.

- Give yourself ample time to shop. When rushing we make mistakes we'll end up paying for in the long run. This includes grocery shopping.

- Separate and contain bulk purchases as soon as you bring them home.

- Don't think you're being environmentally conscientious by saving paper and plastic bags. That goes for glass jars, too. That's why you have a recycle bin. Let the trash guy do his job! Besides, if you shop for food every week, there will be more bags every week. Better yet, do as the Europeans do and take your own bag or basket to the store with you.

- The minute something chips or breaks, put it aside to repair or get rid of it immediately. Remember, your life now is about quality.

- Put a limit on how many bins and containers you need and hold to that number no matter what. Just because you can hide something doesn't mean you need it.

- If you try a new product and you don't like it, pitch it or give it to someone at work the next day. That goes for bath, grooming, food, and health products.

- Never settle for an inferior product because it's all you can afford at the time. Save for what you really want—quality. If that means not treating someone to lunch, limiting your long-distance phone calls, or watching TV instead of renting a video, so be it.

- Out of sight does not mean out of clutter. Don't put souvenirs where you can't see them because you can't decide what to do with them. If you're ambivalent about something, then you don't need it.

- Get in the habit of returning unwanted purchases within a week's time. If you don't, you never will. How do you think book-of-the-month clubs make most of their money? People are too lazy to return things.

- Don't keep books and other nonnecessities to give to someone you rarely run into. Mail the thing and get it out of the house.

- When the new phone book comes, get rid of the old one.

- Keep a vigilant eye on what you really use versus what you thought you'd use. I kept an electric can opener for six years before I realized I never used it.

- Purge your vocabulary of the expression "It's perfectly good." Because it's usually followed by "So I'll keep it." Dig?

- Finish what you start and be leery of complicated long-term projects.

- Don't live in the future. While healthy anticipation is always good, don't think of where you're living as temporary. Get those pictures hung. Paint the place if you want to, and really live there in the "now." You might upgrade someday, but that's later, not now. Be proud of what you have. Embrace it and make it the very best you can.

- Once you are clutter free, pass this book on to someone who needs it.

IN CONCLUSION

There's no question the world is changing rapidly. Some of this change is within our control, but much of it seems thrust upon us. We can either view change with fear or welcome it with a sense of excitement and wonder. For me, change has always brought with it the opportunity, privilege, and permission to reinvent myself! While we cannot control the change in the world, we can take charge of it within our own homes. The first step is to purge what no longer has meaning for us so we can make room for a meaningful life ahead.

We are at an unusual moment in time. Sometimes I feel stretched across generations, between the multitasking, high-technology one I'm trying to understand today and the unfathomable, accelerated world my nephew will inherit. It is even more reason to make honest choices about how we live now. Through clarification we find balance and order, and that is something we can control.

Simplifying our lives is the greatest gift we can give ourselves, and it begins with getting rid of our clutter. It's a physically conscious act that begins with emptying a drawer and continues with a new lease on life. This does not mean there is no longer room within a well-ordered home for sentiment, spirituality, or tradition. These are values we've brought forward with us as human beings since creation, and it's up to us to pass on these values to the next generation. That the next generation will never sit at a typewriter or spin an LP doesn't mean they won't be inspired by words or be moved by beautiful music. They'll just do it in a different way.

With personal time becoming the great prize, where you spend it should please the senses, fill the soul, and quell the fear. Because where there is fear, there is no creativity!

Make the choice. What do you still connect with from the past? What do you really use presently? And what in the future will you really need?

The mental interior always matches your home's interior, and when you change one, the other changes, too. If we are how we live, then get busy making it about who you want to be.

LET'S REVIEW

LAYER 1
ASSESS & SCHEDULE

 This layer is designed to get you mentally ready to change your life. Here, the whole house, from attic to basement, needs to be assessed for you to have a clear picture of what the job at hand really entails. This prevents the domino effect, where every room is torn up at the same time and you become helplessly overwhelmed. With a clear vision, realistic timeline, and workable budget, you're ready for the next layer.

LAYER 2
DETACH & PURGE

 In this stage, we ask you to go through your home as though you were a visitor and to detach yourself emotionally from your stuff. This third-person attitude will help tremendously when the time comes to let go.

LAYER 3
RECLAIM & UPDATE

 Once you've assessed what goes (bye-bye, now) and what stays in each room, it's time to reclaim spaces that have been unlivable until now because of bad planning or clutter. This is also the time to assess the things that you will keep, pending minor updating. Whether the item needs repainting or reupholstering, the key is determining whether the outcome would be worth the effort.

LAYER 4
SORT & CONTAIN

 Here, we separate the utilitarian from the decorative, and the things you don't want to see from those you do. This will give you a clear idea of what needs to be contained and how you'll contain it. In this section, drawers and closets are repurposed to contain the stuff you simply can't live without.

LAYER 5

DESIGN & BUILD

Once you've effectively sorted and contained, it's time to focus on what goes where. Building wall-to-wall shelving can stretch space to make every inch count. But we'll also see that if you can't build out, you can build up. Overhead ledges, bookcases, closets, window seats, and cubbies can now be assembled to display or conceal objects. If this is done well, what was once simply clutter can actually help redefine space, enhance flow, and add design elements to your living environment.

LAYER 6

ARRANGE & DISPLAY

This is the fun part. Now it's time to blend storage containers with decorative objects for maximum visual impact. The art of display comes into play as principles of uniformity and symmetry add balance and drama to your home.

LAYER 7

CEASE & MAINTAIN

Congratulations. Your home is beautifully organized and clutter free. Now your job is to keep it that way. Just because you've picked up extra space does not mean you must fill it. If you don't understand that streamlining is a way of life, your home will get out of control before you know it. A systematic, monthly purging should now go into effect. Acquire only to upgrade! If you find a better widget, get rid of the one you had.

With times so rapidly changing, the way you live today may be completely different from the way you will live ten years from now. In the past decade we've learned to take buildings full of data and condense the information down to a compact disk. We can speak to anyone anywhere in the world while driving a car. We can even take pictures of ourselves while we talk to them.

ROOM MAKEOVERS

You know how directions for recipes, computers, and practically everything else always tell you to read them all the way through before beginning? Remember how I, at the beginning of the Seven Layers, asked you to read them all the way through before beginning? Good for you. Here's why.

Like many things, clearing the clutter from your life and putting your house in order, both literally and figuratively, is a process. Processes by definition are fluid and often continuous. This is certainly true of our lives and therefore naturally true of our homes. So it follows that the organization process is not a cut-and-dried, step-by-step thing. Of course it happens in stages, and ideally in the seven layers I've described here, but I know that you may decide something in Layer Three (Reclaim & Update) that just doesn't work by the time you get to Layer Five (Design & Build).

I know that with some areas or rooms you may go straight to Layer Five and partway to Layer Six (Arrange & Display) before having totally figured out Layer Four (Sort & Contain). That's okay. Don't let adherence to method interfere with achieving the desired result. This is your home, after all, not a mathematical equation.

What I do want you to do is have your priorities clear. And those priorities are clearing the clutter from your house (and your life) to make room for the home (and

the life) you want. Layers One (Assess & Schedule) and Two (Detach &
Purge) are nonnegotiable. You with me? After that we're a little more
flexible. The layers are designed to help you organize your thoughts
and determine your plan of action.

In the room makeovers that follow you'll see we spared you the
play-by-play of us going through sock drawers and garages, but trust
us, we did! We generally begin with Layer Three, discussing how and
where to reclaim space and when (and when not) to recycle and
update furniture. We then move back and forth among Layers Four,
Five, and Six, because that's how it seemed easiest to explain to you
how the room came together. As you begin to see how the layers
work, they will become instinctual and second nature, so that what
once seemed a difficult and mechanical process becomes a natural
and intuitive one. Enjoy!

SUPER STUDIO

In this studio apartment makeover we begin with our newly purged environment, ready to make more effective use of the entire space and some of the existing furniture. This room has to function better as a living room, dining room, office, and bedroom. Our mission is to make a more distinct division between these areas while creating a lot more storage in each place.

While many of our room makeovers mainly deal with Layers Five and Six, this one reaches all the way to Layer Three, Reclaim & Update. There is also a ton of sorting and containing (Layer Four) going on, to fill all the new bookcases (Layer Five, Design & Build), which we of course tastefully arrange with our now well-organized essential items and personal objects (Layer Six, Arrange & Display).

Let's start with the living room conversation area. It's all talk and no show! The furniture itself is modern and unadorned, which is good. And we love it arranged away from the walls, leaving the walls free for more important things. "When in doubt, go bigger" plays well here with the dual-function, oversize ottoman. The choice of two club chairs versus a love seat is far more practical, seating two people comfortably versus one and a half uncomfortably. The sofa, though in need of a new slipcover, is well positioned as a separation device between the living area and the bedroom. But it seems adrift in the room with nothing to anchor it visually. While a table drawn up to its back might help, there really isn't much space to accommodate both a writing table or desk *and* a chair. There's also no room for reading lamps.

As for the room's focal point—the TV and audio speakers? Ugh. While we love the idea that they sit atop an Ikea Lack shelf unit turned unconventionally on its side, we're not crazy about the big black speakers staring us in the face. There's little room for CDs, videos, and the like. Since the wall is already devoted to the equipment, use the whole dang wall, I say.

BEFORE

The two bookcases against the window wall also seem a bit lonely. They should connect to each other somehow to help create a more effective barrier between the living space and the bedroom. Remember, just because they're designed to go against a wall doesn't mean they have to.

Now on to the bedroom. You gotta sleep, right? But not all day. In the waking hours, can't the bedroom look more like a sitting room or den? If an average set of double doors measures only five feet, why does the opening to that area have to be so big and boring? Why is there a lot of wasted space above the bed, little storage, and no side tables?

As for the office area, the workstation is cool. But all by itself it's lonely against the white walls, and there's still about three feet of valuable wall space not being used. Where do family photos go?

The dining area's table and chairs seem dated and not as sophisticated as the blond workstation they're living with.

LIGHT A-PEEL

You'll notice we've added several track lights to the walls. But guess what—the tracks are actually peel-and-stick and plug into any wall socket. They also come with various styles of shades to customize them to your interior—hello! See the Resources on page 170.

But we love the shape, and the chairs are sturdy and just the right size. So it might be worth a little elbow grease to save them.

And what about color? All-white walls are a real mood-killer in any space. Most people think that a studio apartment can't handle anything more aggressive, but once we make the changes to maximize the wall space, we're not going to see much of the paint. I'm thinking a deep flannel gray would really make those blond bookcases and the neutral upholstery pop.

Overall the room is off to a good start, but it's not the great room it could be. The space needs drama and innovative ways to deliberately distinguish one living area from the next while maintaining the room's flow. It needs storage, big time, and the containers we choose will have to contribute to the modern effect. And since we're going to be moving stuff around anyway and everything is already purged, now might be the time to paint—a good way to initiate change while getting the creative juices flowing.

While the paint's drying, let's figure out what's needed in terms of further storage units and containers. A quick spin in cyberspace may spark the imagination.

Make a list of what you'll need first, not what you think you can afford. Budget is a real creativity killer. Get your imagination cooking first. Create a vision of how you want the space to feel, then stick to your guns. When it comes to budget, remember, (a) you're investing in your new life and (b) you're totally worth it. The money you spend now is the start-up cost necessary to move forward into a very cool future.

UPTOWN STU-STU-STUDIO

We're all done, so let me take you on a little tour, okay? Let's start in the living area. We loved the shelf unit on its side and decided to do it again. We built two plywood boxes to encase the speakers and painted them a light gray to complement the deeper gray walls. These act as supports for another IKEA Lack shelf unit on top, linking one box to the other, leaving ample room between the speaker boxes for the TV. But where is it? Well, we wanted the new unit to have the feeling of a fireplace, so we added a door that we hinged to the left speaker box and covered with a mirror, not only to reflect the space but also to double the light coming from our candle garden. At night it adds a romantic

LEFT With the bed turned lengthwise against the wall, it made for a smart-looking daybed that you don't mind viewing from the living area. A collection of black-and-white photos, reoccurring throughout the space, adds height and drama. Illuminated by the peel-and-stick track lighting, the wall now tells a great story.

ambience. For TV viewing, remove the candle garden, open the door, and there it is. So cool!

Estimates for reupholstering the sofa came to $900. Ouch. At IKEA, however, we found a simple, sleek sofa for $399. That was more like it. It was kind of dorm-room-looking, but we had other plans for it. To visually anchor it as the dividing element between the living area and the bedroom, we encased it on three sides with ready-to-assemble (30-inch-high) bookcases. This provided not only storage but a surface on which to place lamps. It's also handy as a buffet surface close to the dining room table and at minimum, a great place to set down your book, beverage, or both. Love that.

And we're walking . . . and we're walking . . . and now—drumroll, please—we present: a study by day and a delicious bedroom by night. Yep, we gave the bed the same treatment we gave the sofa. Bookcases provide storage, act as end tables, support lamps, and tie the living room and bedroom together into one cohesive design. Encasing the bed turns it into a focal point that's tailored and multifunctional, all for less than $200. Yahoo!

Remember the lonely but oh-so-stylish office hutch? To maximize the wall space, we flanked it with two corner towers to add storage and a place for family photos. The matching credenza now acts as a place to store dishes, napkins, and other entertaining paraphernalia.

FAR RIGHT Looking from the bedroom out into the living area, these bookcases (visible only from inside the bedroom) have been reserved for personal bed and bath items such as towels, linens, and containers that hold everything from jewelry to rolled neckties.

BEAUTY AND THE BOOKCASE

As we discussed earlier and as you will see repeated throughout the book, dividing space with bookcases can really save the day. Seven-foot bookcases placed back-to-back and perpendicular to the wall create a deliberate entrance into what is now the study by day and the bedroom by night. They also add much needed storage while at the same time adding architectural interest. We took it a step further by adding a curio cabinet to showcase an art-glass collection. So the next time you want a wall where a wall ought to be but can't afford a contractor or the landlord's wrath, fear not: When you move, these walls go with you!

TO BUILD

- We mirrored the ends of the bookcases, leaving space to mount three precut floating glass shelves. They come with their own mounting channels, so installation is a breeze.

- On the floor at the base of each set of bookcases, we placed a plywood cube painted light gray.

- We then built 4-inch-thick headers to go above the shelves at the top of the bookcases, and into those placed two battery-operated stick-on lights. So for an additional cost of about $80 per side, we were able to customize the inexpensive, nondescript cases into what is now the focal point of the entire apartment.

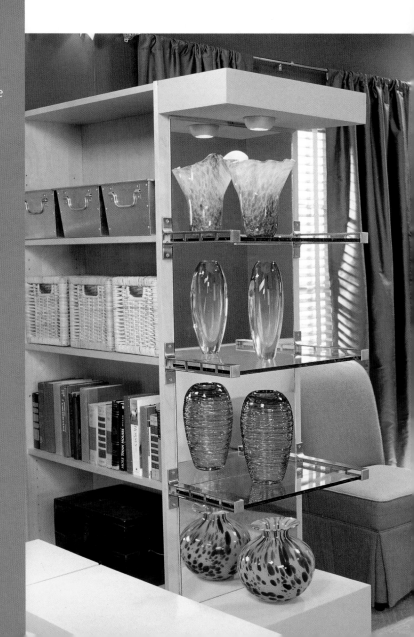

Love Note from Layer 4, Sort & Contain

Let's observe how well-chosen storage containers actually promote good design. You'll note that throughout this space, metal bins and square banana baskets (that's what Ikea calls them) are dispersed uniformly at the same height and on the same shelf from bookcase to bookcase. This adds a graphic element and a sense of order to each area. While these containers add valuable hidden storage, they also provide an easy way to decorate open shelving. Even the books are placed together on the third shelf of each bookcase rather than randomly here and there. This cuts down on the visual noise. With all the shelves so in your face, simplicity and repetition are key. And remember, there's power in mass. One element repeated fifteen times throughout a space makes a deliberate statement and tells all who enter that there was a specific thought process at work here.

We went all out in this space to show you as many storage ideas as we could—maybe too many, but I hope you get our point. Storage and order can be beautiful!

DOABLE REDO

The early American table had everything going for it except its color (see the BEFORE picture on page 97). After a light sanding and a coat of primer, the same light gray paint used elsewhere was slapped on and dried within two hours. But the chairs (who wants to do those with a brush?) got spray painted in the same color. A coat of polyurethane to the tabletop now fully integrated the work/dining table into the chic uptown apartment.

LEFT Mixing containers with accessories can create great vignettes while adding lifts and levels for visual interest. Uniformity in color also helps visually coordinate a tableau.

MEALS ON WHEELS

A big part of stretching space is looking for opportunities to add "multifunction" to as many things as you can. When I sit at my design table and start sketching, I'm always asking myself, "Can this item do more than one thing? Will wheels give me more flexibility? How might I incorporate more storage?" In my book *Small Spaces* I talk a lot about ways to maximize space by using two very important techniques: building from wall to wall and building up.

This dining room is located off a kitchen that can be seen from a living room and worse, from the front door. Obviously, the round table and chairs squeezed into this weird little area don't cut it. Wasted overhead space remains empty, while a small chest further intrudes on what is already a tiny area. By the time we finished all seven layers of organization, not only had we increased the seating to accommodate *six* people comfortably, but we had also gained a ton of storage. How? Well, I just told you, silly—by building wall to wall and building up.

BEFORE

AFTER

ENSCONCED

We made these wall sconces for about $10 each, but their impact is worth so much more, don't you agree? Hung all together they look stunning, showing again how one little motif repeated in mass can make a major statement.

- Remove the glass from ready-made picture frames. Paint the frames chocolate brown.

- Have mirrors cut to fit the frames.

- Coat the mirrors with floral tinting spray. Sprays are available from the craft store (we liked chartreuse).

- In the center of the lower part of each frame, attach a candle cup (also a craft store item).

TABLE FOR SIX, PLEASE

Here's Layer Five, Design & Build, at work:

- The banquette is a big box open in front to accommodate baskets for storing napkins, place mats, and all that other dining stuff.

- A 3 × 8-foot hollow-core door is attached to the top of the box, and a piece of foam is cut to fit on top.

- The cushion is upholstered in brown velvet, with coordinating pillows.

- The table is one hollow-core door for the top and another cut in half for the sides.

- We added wheels to the table to make it easier to get in and out.

- Inexpensive upholstered chairs, their slipcovers dyed brown, complete the seating arrangement.

As with many of our ideas, our Layer Five (Design & Build) inspiration came from the experts. In this case, we took our cues from restaurant planners who have to have as much seating as possible. A variation on the banquette concept seemed to be the ticket. Banquettes can be built wall to wall, eliminating the need for chair space. With that idea, and a photo from a smart little Amsterdam hotel, we were off and running.

First we had to Reclaim & Update (Layer Three) the small, underscale window. The framing left by a former window was still visible through the plaster, so we reframed the window at its original size. While the upper portion of the window would not be usable, a great wooden blind would cover the top portion and no one would be the wiser. We then wanted an overhead display area, so we installed a shelf along one wall and continued it around the corner to the window wall and on around to the other side of the window. Its thickness and invisible mounting brackets gave the space a modern feel.

With most of the wall construction finished, we painted the space in a two-tone scheme that gave the space the illusion of height.

For Layer Six (Arrange & Display) we wanted to add romance and drama, which we got from wonderful sconces (see "Ensconced" on page 108) and large rice-paper globes. Glass and black-and-green accessories completed this little jewel box of a room.

This same banquette made with a full-size core door could easily accommodate a twin bed. Add velvet curtains to the entrance and you have an instant guest room. Another slam-dunk in a space that seemed hopeless.

Because we can, here's another breakfast nook makeover. Here, you can see the magic of Layer Three (Reclaim & Update). We used color and faux finishes to take this 1940s turret breakfast nook over the top. You can tell how small the space is by the scale of the chrome dinette set that underwhelms the room. We began the transformation by painting the walls in a kitschy bamboo pattern and bringing balloon shades down from the ceiling for window treatments. The doors on the front of the built-in hutch were faux-finished to replicate old mirroring. To that we added moldings. We loved the faux finish so much we also did it on the wooden tabletop, which was a flea-market find. Add an over-the-top chandelier, and another small space makes a big impression.

BEFORE

AFTER

SHIP-TO-SHORE BEDROOM

My former vacation house overlooked the ocean in Manhattan Beach, California. Like many homes where the real estate is hot, mine was a very vertical affair, with one room smaller than the next. I had a real challenge decorating the small, oddly shaped master suite. Since this was a new house for me, implementing the layers of organization began with Layer Five, Design & Build, and Layer Six, Arrange & Display. Layer Four, Sort & Contain, was more or less integral to the process, as you'll see.

Fitting a queen-size bed into the room would leave little space for much else, so storage ideas were key. Making things worse was the fact that there was only one uninterrupted wall in the whole room. I also needed a place to write, which is why I bought the house in the first place. So I came up with an idea to combine the bed with the desk.

Beyond the bed, I made a narrow table to go under the window. Again, a fiberboard box was constructed with two cubbyholes for decorative storage. It was faux-finished like the bed and set with matching lamps and a sailboat. We are at the shore after all.

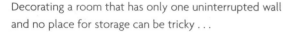

Decorating a room that has only one uninterrupted wall and no place for storage can be tricky . . .

BEFORE

BEFORE

AFTER

. . . so when you finally get one, make every inch count!

BEFORE

Now what to do about a dresser? Clotheshorse that I am because of showbiz and all, I needed room. So I built two cubby towers sized to fit the baskets I'd purchased first. Never do it the other way around; that's why Sort & Contain (Layer Four) comes before Design & Build (Layer Five). To connect these towers so they'd look built in, I used shelves with invisible mounts and installed an overhead shelf all around the room except for the bed wall. Once it was in place the shelf gave me room for forty matching baskets, which added great texture to the space. What I also loved is that the baskets could be brought anywhere you needed them for easy rummaging.

Once I moved into the room, I realized there was a fishbowl effect at night, since the bedroom window looked directly into the living room across the alley. I needed a window treatment for privacy, but I still wanted filtered light. So I found ready-made cotton curtains with chrome grommets, which I threaded with cable as a curtain rod, and that was that. I liked it so much I used the same treatment throughout most of the house.

ID, PLEASE

What I didn't love about my forty identical baskets was that I found myself playing the match game every time I needed something. I finally attached leather luggage tags to them to identify the contents. They looked great and I knew what was where.

TRAY CHIC

This sliding desk worked like a charm except for a very important feature we forgot to include. I made pasta for myself and was going to eat in bed while watching TV. When I got up during the show, I pushed the desk to the foot of the bed and it kept going like a freight train. I spent the rest of the evening cleaning red pasta sauce off my new white carpet. Lessen learned? Put a stop at the end of the track! Here's the rest of the story:

- The bed platform is made of fiberboard and faux-finished to look like veneer.

- For the headboard, we created a tall box with two openings for decorative storage.

- The base of the platform is covered in batting and upholstered in brown microsuede.

- On either side of the bed platform we attached aluminum track, the same used for sliding closet doors. For stops, we nailed small blocks of wood at the end of each track.

- We constructed a desk of fiberboard slightly wider than the width of the bed so it would slide over the bed.

Several primitive wooden trunks clustered at the foot of the bed are used for storing off-season clothes. Since there was no wall space for more surfaces, I used two pedestal tables with round glass tops. An arrangement of wooden boxes, leather hatboxes, and accessories gives the feeling of a men's haberdashery and stores everything from loose change to jewelry.

The techniques used in my room were adapted in an even tinier guest room on the lower floor, which also had only one uninterrupted wall. Storage was not as much of an issue, since overnight guests could use the built-in closet. But the bed really was about all that would fit here, too, so I had to really play it up.

Both of these rooms came out so well I thought I'd move them to the big L.A. house when I got an offer on the beach house I couldn't refuse. On moving day, we realized that there was no way to get the beds out of the rooms. I'd built the proverbial ark in the basement. So God bless my crew—they came in with sledgehammers and demolished both beds. Lesson learned? If you want to take it with you, keep everything modular, baby!

A BED AND BEYOND

This might be the hardest-working bed west of the Mississippi. Here's what I mean:

- A huge arch made of fiberboard contains two inside cubbyholes. One houses the portable telephone, the other an alarm clock.

- Dimmer switches control the recessed light overhead and the wall sconces.

- The headboard is six pieces of quarter-inch plywood wrapped in batting and covered in yellow microsuede.

- The footboard is another, smaller arch also made out of fiberboard. It doubles as a desk or workspace.

- Underneath is a fiberboard box on wheels. The front is upholstered in matching microsuede, with two towel racks as handles. The pedestal bed doubles as an ottoman and as a place to store towels and linens, which the small adjoining bathroom could not hold.

BEFORE

AFTER

YACHT CHIC PUBLIC SPACES

Now, if you think my beach house bedrooms were tricky, my public spaces were even trickier. Sticking with my yacht chic, ship-to-shore theme, I decided to build as much into the room as possible, for the simple reason that it would maximize every inch of space. As with the Ship-to-Shore Bedroom chapter preceding this one, this was a new house for me. You'll see Layer Three in action, though, as we reclaim both spaces and furniture in some very interesting ways. The kitchen, of course, is Layer Four (Sort & Contain) city. The rest is all about Layers Five and Six. Ahoy! Oh, I mean, enjoy!

KITCHEN BEFORE

The entire space was quite narrow, and with the ocean view being the big story, I decided to install mirrors on all the walls facing the windows. Not only did this give the optical illusion of doubling the space, but it also gave me a 360-degree view of the Pacific.

LIVING ROOM BEFORE

LIVING ROOM AFTER

More living room seating—without blocking the view—was achieved with a backless settee and two swivel chairs flanking a table under the window next to the fireplace. That way, people could turn to the fireplace or the view in the opposite direction. Acting as both footrest and coffee table, six square ottomans formed a compact and versatile rectangle.

The tiny dining room separated the living room from the open kitchen, making each room visible from the next. There was no space to store anything, and furniture placement was challenging. If you faced the fireplace, you couldn't see the view, which I had paid dearly for. And where do you put the TV, for heaven's sake? Normally, I don't advocate putting a TV in the living room, but I also didn't want to tromp way down to my bedroom to watch it, or worse, make my company pile onto the bed . . . don't even go there! The dining room had no place to store dining stuff, nor was there a bar, save for the kitchen. To complicate things further, I had a grand piano and no place to put it but the dining room. So much for a dining room table. Bummer.

The kitchen had only two real problems: It was completely open and had very little counter space. Therefore, it needed to be ultraorganized. This really did me a favor, as I

KITCHEN AFTER

The grommeted cotton curtains suspended on cables were used to create further definition of space while playing up the sailboat theme.

was forced to purge five years' worth of collected kitchen clutter. Just the essentials would do here. I was in desperate need of a pot rack, but knew I shouldn't hang it in the middle of the kitchen with nothing underneath it—*bong!*

Beginning with the living room, I designed a restaurant-style banquette, with storage underneath. A triangle pedestal in the corner allows two or more people to sit there comfortably. One arm of the banquette would also be the top of a low storage cabinet that would fit against the new built-in dining room bar.

With the living room under control, I turned my attention to the dining room, where nightclubs were my inspiration. I simply could not give up my piano. So I turned it into the dining room table by designing a top that would accommodate six guests. We added six bar-height chairs and said, "Bring on the martinis!"

Even the kitchen got ample seating with three counter-height chairs and a 1940s aluminum park bench. This seating makes the kitchen feel more like a "room room" instead of a "kitchen room"—which is especially good when the kitchen is so open to the rest of the house. I went to a restaurant-supply store and had a narrow stainless-steel table made to be used as a kitchen island. Over it I hung a pot rack with built-in lights that illuminate the constantly used island.

Applying Layer Six (Arrange & Display) to this space was a lot of fun. Primitive bowls and giant black concrete containers filled with shells played against the sleek chrome and helped ground the space visually. But should you ever move oceanside, beware—everything metal rusts!

Because so many of the inherent problems had been solved, I later sold the house the first day it was on the market, and at a nice profit. So don't be afraid to invest in your home. When you do things right, it goes right to the bottom line.

LEFT To connect one wall visually with the other, I designed a large soffit with recessed lighting, which would join one set of cabinets to the other. Once I had designed everything, I handed the plans over to my able carpenter, Bill Newkirk, who would build the pieces off-site and assemble them in the house.

ABOVE A pair of pedestals and two torso-shaped lamps with white shades inspired the chrome-and-white element, which was picked up in all the other lamps throughout the space.

RIGHT A grand piano converts into a grand dining room table.

OFFICE BY DAY, GUEST ROOM BY NIGHT

I know many of you simply do not have enough space to dedicate one room or even one area entirely to a home office. Often, the office ends up in the guest bedroom. So, with that in mind, we set out to create a home office by day and a guest bedroom by night, which comes from the heart of Layer Three, Reclaim & Update. And nothing says this can't be done in your own bedroom, either.

There's nothing really wrong with this room, but it just isn't living up to its potential. There's little storage available for guests, and while the bed is fine, it has no drama. The

THE GRACIOUS HOST

A guest room that looks like you put some thought into it makes a strong statement about your hospitality and is one of the nicest ways to express a spirit of warmth and generosity toward others. As trite as it sounds, little things really do mean a lot, especially to your guests.

BEFORE

AFTER

For the window treatment, we loved the idea of a sailing ship, so we attached wooden swing arms to the window casings and rigged them with panels of white canvas. Stainless-steel ship-to-shore droplights highlight the "sails." A small settee at the end of the bed and a few well-chosen accessories finish the space.

AFTER

office area needs to be better organized so as not to intrude visually on the guest area. (Yoo-hoo! Layer Four, Sort & Contain!) I think the upholstered chair is a nice size and shape for the space, but the sweet little print dates it (call on Layer Three again). The bookcases (Layer Five, Design & Build) are a good idea, but they're not well decorated (Layer Six, Arrange & Display). Containers will hide some of the office stuff and make the space more guest friendly, especially if you don't want them seeing how much your mortgage payment is.

The rest of the furnishings are a bit disjointed, too. Although there seems to be a slight lean toward a "shore" look, nothing is really taking us there beyond the bedspread, which I like.

To play up the shore theme, we painted the walls an ocean-inspired blue with white trim. This would become the perfect backdrop for many of the fabrics and accessories already in the room, including the neutral-colored carpet. Starting under the L-shaped window, we used the two bedside chests and repainted them with a quick whitewash. These were then placed to the far left and under the window to support an interlocking shelf made from a double thickness of fiberboard. We built a half-circle pedestal out of plywood, and covered it with tambour (vertical slats backed with canvas), which you'll see later on our shore-

inspired coffee table. This supported the shelf in its center and would act as a great writing desk for guests—thus keeping them out of the office area.

We sent the hand-me-down chair out to be re-covered in a green tweed ($275) and drew it up to the desk, getting rid of the faux Windsor chair that was obviously made for a dining room table.

With the office surround looking so great, we decided to turn our attention to the bed. But this time, over the bead-board wall treatment we placed three pieces of van, wrapped them with cotton batting, and covered them with terry-cloth towels. This created a spalike feeling for the bed and a comfortable backrest to boot. We attached small disk lights to the interior of the bed, placing the switch conveniently next to the bed. The existing bedspread looked wonderful accented with decorative pillows.

This once ho-hum and sterile space was completely transformed into a handsome, versatile, and organized shore-inspired guest room and home office for a very reasonable sum. Proof that architecture, storage, and design can come together by using ready-made items in unconventional ways. So much of the drama is about adding height and scale and thinking outside the box.

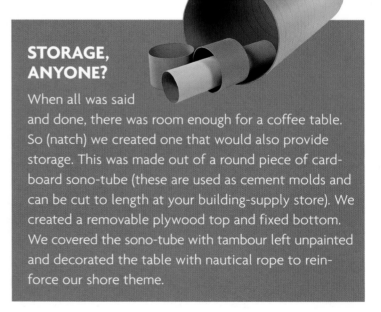

STORAGE, ANYONE?

When all was said and done, there was room enough for a coffee table. So (natch) we created one that would also provide storage. This was made out of a round piece of cardboard sono-tube (these are used as cement molds and can be cut to length at your building-supply store). We created a removable plywood top and fixed bottom. We covered the sono-tube with tambour left unpainted and decorated the table with nautical rope to reinforce our shore theme.

INSTANT OFFICE

A couple of bookcases, a door, and some molding create a cozy and contained workspace.

■ On either side of the existing table we placed bookcases with the shelves facing out.

■ We then cut a sheet of bead board and attached it directly to the inside wall joining the two bookcases together. This made them look built in and added to the nautical feel.

■ We mounted two lights to the underside of a hollow-core door and trimmed it out on three sides with white crown molding, to fit directly on top of the two bookcases.

■ Ready-made shelves are arranged with pictures, decorative storage containers, and office organizers.

■ We left the space open, but a pair of curtains could easily be added to discourage guests' prying eyes.

OFFICE POLITICS: DIVIDE AND CONCUR

A few years ago, we started getting a lot of people calling us to ask if we had cool ideas for people sharing home office space. We found out that many couples who had reached retirement age weren't ready to stop being productive. Sometimes these couples, set in their ways, were afraid that working together in the same room as their spouse might drive them crazy. Later we began to receive e-mails from young couples who worked outside the home during the day but still needed communal workspace. They were also concerned that things might get too close for comfort.

In shared workspaces, there must be well-defined common areas as well as a clear-cut workstation for each per-

BEFORE

BEFORE

AFTER

son. As in many traditional male/female relationships, each person wants an inspiring environment that reflects his or her sensibilities. This can easily lead to typical Mars versus Venus disputes if these shared work environments aren't kept gender-neutral. A home workspace can promote good design and be multifunctional if proper attention to space planning is well thought out before money has been spent and the two of you are no longer speaking. With that in mind, we designed this makeover to help illustrate great ideas for a space that is luxurious enough for her, yet tailored enough for him.

Take a look at this study before the makeover. Here, two people are trying to share the same workspace. Clearly, the two oversize chairs at the opposite end of the room are taking up valuable space that could very easily contain a second workstation. There is little to no well-defined common area and the furniture that is there seems out of place.

Many home offices are considered dumping grounds for chairs and tables that don't fit anywhere else. Devoid of color and any real decoration, these rooms end up low on charm. They ultimately become uninspiring and therefore stressful to be in for hours at a time. In many cases, it's the lack of up-front space planning, not the lack of space, that robs the room of its function. This is why the first layer of organization, Assess & Schedule, is so important.

We redid this entire office—not by removing what was there, but by making the space work more effectively. We began by painting the space a good, unisex background color—a deep regency green. The trim was kept white, but for additional charm, we added more—especially around

AFTER

the focal-point window in the center of the room. Using a wooden appliqué (from the craft store) and several feet of molding, we created a handsome window pediment bridging the two windows. This added substance and instant architectural interest to the space.

Next, we wanted to create one single element that would act as a unifying device throughout the space. We decided that decorative fluting would play up the regency style, so in each corner of the room we affixed fluted half-round columns stained a deep mahogany. These decorative elements were made from foam pipe insulation, secured with plaster to pie-wedge shapes of sono-tube, and nailed to several pie-wedge shapes of plywood. (Sono-tube can be cut to order at your building-supply store.) We liked the look so much that we continued it on many of the support mechanisms in the room.

To flank the new window treatment, we purchased ten floating IKEA Lack shelves (five for each side) and secured them to the walls with the invisible mounting brackets that come with then. Once those were up, we created the illusion that the entire collection of shelves was actually a freestanding étagère by placing tambour-covered (PVC pipe sections) at each corner.

We moved the table under the center window to serve as a common work surface, to be used there or rolled into either workstation. In the center of the room, we built another common work surface that—guess what?—doubles as a storage unit.

Modern oversize lights were dropped from the ceiling over each work area, while a series of wall sconces illuminated the architecture of the room. And there was still room for the small regency table and an oversize upholstered chair.

So what was once a lackluster space with only one work area now has become a dual office with several well-defined areas, divided by a multifunctional unit that can be shared by him and her. It can be used for work or entertaining and has a sleek, clean feel that is neither feminine nor masculine—ideal for the couple that works together, and assuring that now they'll stay together.

The art of placement adds a sense of order to an ordinary set of shelves.

DECO DELIGHT

This very cool work surface/storage unit divides the space and can also serve as a bar or buffet.

- We began with five open plywood boxes, three in graduating sizes for the base, and two of equal size for the top. With the smallest at the bottom, three were stacked on top of one another and bolted together from the inside with L-shape brackets.

- The largest box was designed to hold the hollow-core door top. It and the small box were painted black, while the rest of the boxes were painted the same color as the shelves opposite them.

- For the top, we attached the remaining two boxes and installed them with the openings facing out to hold baskets and additional storage.

- The upper and lower units were joined together with four lengths of plumber's pipe and six mounting flanges. The pipes were wrapped with dark-stained tambour, bringing the same fluted detail into the center of the room.

This versatile room divider makes for a great buffet.

LEFT Here's a cool dividing device to separate one small office area from another. A large sheet of Plexiglas sandwiched between stair-stepped book/magazine cases offers privacy but still allows each person visual space.

BELOW, LEFT AND RIGHT An open box header concept is used as part of the built-in desk. Long boxes were attached to the wall above and below the window. The same type of hollow-core door table we used in our breakfast nook (page 109) was painted black and slipped in underneath the box below the window. Below the table we also added two more boxes—the large on top and the smaller below. When the desk moves away from the wall, it reveals an open storage area underneath.

PASS-THROUGH SPACES: THE LONG HALL

Almost every home or apartment has a hallway, usually leading to back bedrooms. Narrow, windowless, and generally thought of as simply pass-through spaces, they remain for the most part undecorated ... and unclaimed! Hello, Layer Three, Reclaim & Update. Despite the hall's long and narrow awkwardness, it's still 16 to 18 feet of uninterrupted

BEFORE

AFTER

We painted the hall a deep tan color and the ceiling two shades lighter. When the paint dried, we laid a photo-laminate sheet of vinyl over a nasty beat-up floor to give the illusion of new hardwood floors. We added a runner later so not much of the "fake" floor would end up showing.

space—valuable space in which to tell your stories. Multiply that by an average height of 8 feet and you've got more than 200 square feet of decorating potential! Did I get your attention? All righty, then.

So cash in those frequent-flier miles as we take a trip to a Spanish bungalow in Southern California and to a two-bedroom walk-up in Manhattan to get some great ideas for pass-through spaces. As with most hallways, the operative word is "narrow," and the narrower the better.

We re-created this boxcar of a back hallway from photos sent to us by a photographer living in Manhattan. He explained in a letter that he'd run out of display space for his ethnic art collection and that his home also doubles as his gallery. It seems we don't have much to do with Layer Four (Sort & Contain), but Layers Five (Design & Build) and Six (Arrange & Display) come into play big time. Watch this.

In our workshop, following his floor plan, we created the 12-foot hallway you see here. Again, the concept of building up became our mantra. We then set out to design a wall treatment that would incorporate four ledges that would traverse the walls of the hallway. On the long walls we

decided we could intrude only on the space about four inches from each side. The back of the hall, which once housed a small three-drawer chest, could accommodate standard 1-foot shelves that would butt into the left and right picture ledges. This would visually connect the horizontal lines throughout the space. It was this graphic, striped effect that would become the design icon for our "made in Manhattan" hallway makeover.

STEP-BY-STEP SHELF

- After measuring the hallway carefully, 1×4-inch pine strips plus 1×1-foot shelves (for the end of the hall) were cut by the guys at our building-supply store, so the pieces were portable enough to lug up in a small elevator.

- We also had the building-supply store guys "rip" (that's what they call sawing—whatever!) twenty pieces of half-inch fiberboard, which is a lightweight wood composite available anywhere plywood is sold. Some of them were cut in half for easier transport; we put them back together during installation.

- Back at the workshop, we painted the pine strips with black semigloss. These would be the picture ledges. We then polyurethaned the fronts of the fiberboard, which intensified their natural honey color and accentuated the sandy texture. This would become the new wall treatment for our back hallway.

- To install the shelves, we worked from the floor up, measuring the walls and using a plumb line to level and mark the walls lightly in chalk. This was the hardest part of the job—and that was easy, if you get my drift—an idiot can do this project. And so we idiots started from the floor and worked our way up to the last ledge, which hit about 2 feet from the ceiling.

- The first black 1×4-inch strip was installed flat against the wall, acting as a baseboard. Next, using fine-finish nails and Liquid Nails, we secured the first strip of polyurethaned fiberboard to rest on the 1-inch black baseboard.

- The black pine strips were then glued and nailed to the exposed edge of the MDF (medium-density fiberboard), creating a 4-inch shelf protruding from the wall. The next piece of MDF was attached above that, and so on. The MDF was a strong support channel, making the photo ledges nice and sturdy. In the back part of the hall this proved vital in adding needed support to the deeper 1-foot shelves.

- We placed mirror tiles as molding (affixed with Mirror Mastic) on the wall just beneath the ceiling.

- On the long walls, mirror tiles were installed in groups of two, leaving a 6-inch gap of exposed wall for inexpensive, adjustable wall sconces. This created an illusion that the ceilings were much higher and the hall was floating in the center of what appeared to be a larger room beyond.

- We liked it so much that we mirrored the two doors as well. We cut the mirror tiles to the same dimensions as each of the raised door panels and "framed" them with black paint. (Mind you, we did this after laying the doors flat so that gravity was not an issue as the Liquid Nails dried.)

With the construction complete and wall sconces installed, it was time to tear in to Layer Six and arrange and display! But wait, how cool would it be to have a place to actually sit in the hallway? *Very cool* is the answer. So we built a plywood box and rested it on another smaller box made from the baseboard/ledge 1×4's. To that we added a cloth-covered piece of foam. Done! Then we decorated ourselves into oblivion—oh my God, so much fun.

What was once a nondescript homage to wasted space now held a collection of more than sixty pieces of art. Our client says that all but three apartments in his building have duplicated his hallway design. I guess imitation *is* the sincerest form of flattery!

HOORAY FOR HALL-YWOOD!

Our line producer, Greg, was so desperate for one of our famous makeovers in his own home that he threatened to put us in the red if we didn't do it . . . so we did it. Never piss off the guy who controls your budget. Since Greg is a show-biz producer, we decided to reflect his love for all things Hollywood.

In a basically dungeonlike back hallway leading to the study, two bedrooms, and a bath, we did our first walk-through to get inspired. In the forties, when this L.A. bunga-low was built, tone-on-tone interiors were the rage. So with that as our springboard, we attacked the hallway.

Painting the space a warm yellow-beige made a huge dif-ference right off the bat. Highlighting the wood trim in crisp, clean white created a subtle contrast that we'd later pick up in the accessories. The deep arched entrance to the hallway needed architectural interest, so we used Anaglypta, a thick wallpaperlike surface treatment, and covered the entrance walls in what appeared to be fine-etched plaster once it was painted. We liked the effect so much that we repeated it far-ther down the hall in the arched niche carved out for the telephone.

ABOVE This little alcove in Greg's home was directly to the right of his front door. We added a great-looking chest, a photo ledge of faux brick, and a large flea-market mirror to open up the space visually. A table lamp and a wall sconce brought light and mood to an otherwise dimly lit, normally wasted space.

BEFORE

BEFORE

AFTER

AFTER

The bathroom door at the end of the hall came complete with an atrocious purple glass window that had "bordello" written all over it. Never mind the Barney-purple tiled bathroom beyond. Anyway, we simply attached a large framed print over the window and it went away. The art of disguise is often key to interior design.

The rest of the job was all about decorating. White ceramics on whitewashed pedestals, plants, art, and up-lights tucked here and there turned this dungeon into a chic, Hollywood-inspired space that ended up being the very inspiration for the remodeling of the rest of the house—who knew?

As a footnote: Greg was one of those people who, because he didn't know what to do with his house, did nothing. When the house was eventually remodeled and decorated, he told us that it literally gave him a new lease on life. He realized that, until we finished it, he really had not begun actually "living" in a home he'd occupied for years. And you could tell it was the truth because something about him changed. There was a sense of pride now visible to the entire production staff. See? By changing your home, you *can* change your life.

COLLEGE COOL

Getting kids into the purging process early is not a bad idea. I know it's often difficult to dictate what should or should not be in your teen's room, but if you can get them involved it starts them off with good habits while helping them to appreciate what they own. Purging also helps them to develop a sense of pride about the things around them— and respect for your things, too.

I also think it's critical to give kids an environment that supports their creativity. If you sense they have an interest in or aptitude for something specific, let that be reflected in their rooms. My nephew Christopher is a wonderful artist. Every time I visit, I give him art supplies, and he has a place in his room where his art stuff is set up. That way, if he gets an inspiration he can respond to it immediately rather than having to organize his materials and risk losing the moment. If a kid loves a particular athlete or musician, rather than taping a poster up on the wall, have it nicely framed for his or her room. It's a great way to take interest and to show that you care.

Beyond such generous but relatively innocuous gestures on your part, it's pretty much hands off Junior's room till he flies the coop. I have seen parents who try to push their taste level on their kids, and it always backfires. While I think you should create opportunities to show you're interested, don't try to give your child the room you never had.

Even if you don't have kids, you'll get some great ideas from this chapter because all the principles can easily adapt to other rooms. We've designed this room as a teenage boy's retreat, but just next door (in the next chapter) is a great room for a teenage girl. These two rooms are actually one space divided by a set of bookcases. After we're done here we'll move over to the adjoining room in the following chapter—no peeking, okay?

A kid's room, or a dorm room, needs to function in several ways, so we'll do a very creative application of Layer

CLOSET STUDIES

Two key missing elements were the closet and the desk. We came up with a way to combine the two.

- For the desktop, we slid a hollow-core door into one of the bookshelves. The other end of the door rested on a two-drawer file cabinet.

- To the right side of the desktop we attached another door and braced it to the wall with two 4-foot pieces of steel pipe and four flanges. This not only kept the door nice and straight in its vertical position, but the pipes also acted as closet rods.

- Four ready-made corner shelves were attached to bridge the closet wall to the window wall on one side and the bookshelves on the other.

We used the backs of the book-cases by attaching a full-length mirror to one and a Peg-Board to another. The mirror helps create the illusion of space, while the Peg-Board provides storage for office supplies and the like.

Three, in reclaiming space and updating some of the exist-ing pieces. There must be a bed, a workstation, a closet, a TV and "chilling" area, and storage, storage, storage (all Layer Four issues).

The heavy lifting begins with Layer Five, Design & Build. We partitioned the room with five bookcases. Two book-cases were bolted together and placed perpendicular to the window wall. An opening was left, providing an entrance into the adjoining room, which would later be fitted with a wooden blind. On the other side of the entrance, following the same line, three more bookcases were bolted together.

The trick was to turn every other one facing into the adjoin-ing room.

Bold wall color adds a sense of intimacy. And while the airplane photos and accessories obviously say "male," with-out the gender-specific accessories, this room could be uni-sex. Another option (budget permitting) could be a sleeper sofa, thus making this an adult space ideal as a den by day and a guest room by night.

As you digest what we've done in this room, let's consider some other really cool ways to create self-contained spaces that kids won't mind spending time in. On to "her" room now!

The cool coffee table was made with wooden CD towers and a painted plywood top. At the back of each CD tower we attached four pipes and flanges to another sheet of plywood painted to match the top. Wheels added roll-around flexibility.

BELOW AND RIGHT New ways
for ready-mades.

A BED-DER DEAL

The bed needed to be a sofa by day but still easily
accessible for sleeping by night, with—ta-da!—ample
storage around and underneath.

■ To elevate it to a comfortable sitting height while
  providing much needed storage, we used two IKEA
  Lack shelf units turned on their sides and parallel to
  each other.

■ To support the mattress, we added what's called a
  futon lade. It's basically several slats of wood bound
  together with strips of fabric.

■ Two more shelf units were placed vertically on both
  sides of the bed, while another turned on its side
  bridged one to the other overhead. This was secured
  to the wall with brackets and then bolted to each of
  the vertical shelf units.

SORORITY SPLENDOR

So this is what's on the other side of that blue sheet! Another wasted space? Yes, but not for long. While we set out to do a girl's dorm room or bedroom, with a more generous use of fabric, the result actually resembled a chic hotel suite. That's a good thing, because this makeover contains great ideas for guest rooms, too.

Our goal was to create a focal-point bed treatment, a generous closet, a dining area, a relax and chill space, and a full workstation, plus storage, storage, storage.

Remember that on the other side of this room is the boy's room, so the bookcases and the window shade entrance are shared by both spaces ... get it?

For the writing desk/workstation we purchased four 30-inch-high bookcases, assembled them, and placed them back-to-back in pairs perpendicular to the wall, about three feet apart. The inward-facing shelves were ideal for keeping stuff organized and out of view. A good old hollow-core door provided the top working surface. Four ready-made CD towers, bolted together back-to-back and placed on the

BEFORE

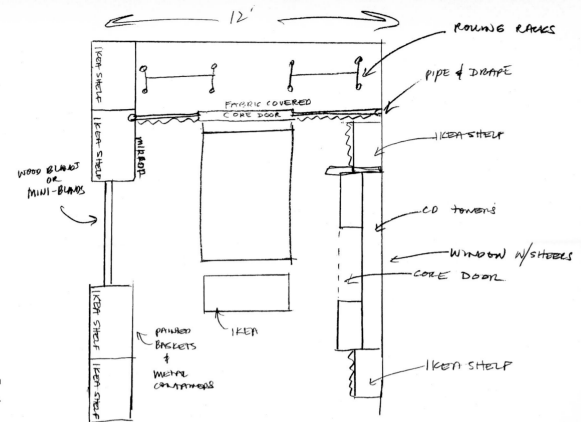

Define how you want your room to work with a sketch.

Labels in sketch: 12', ROLLING RACKS, PIPE & DRAPE, IKEA SHELF, FABRIC COVERED CORE DOOR, IKEA SHELF, WOOD BLINDS OR MINI-BLINDS, MIRROR, CD towers, WINDOW W/SHEERS, CORE DOOR, PAINTED BASKETS & METAL CONTAINERS, IKEA, IKEA SHELF, IKEA SHELF, IKEA SHELF

CURTAIN CLOSET AND HEADBOARD

Our biggest challenge was to create a full closet, which we did similarly to the one in the boy's room in the previous chapter, except that this version created a luxurious wall of fabric. The free-flowing drapes on both sides of the core doors acted as the doors to the closet, and the padded and fabric-covered core doors became a headboard when we simply pushed the head of the bed against them.

- For the headboard, we began with two 4 × 8-foot lightweight hollow-core doors. We nailed them together and covered one side with batting and then with green velvet (which came from ready-made curtains, à la Scarlett O'Hara).

- We then placed the headboard in the back center of the room (fabric side facing out), 4 feet from the wall, and secured it with plumbing pipes and flanges in 4-foot lengths. One was mounted 1½ feet from the top

and the other 3 feet lower. And presto, double-hanging closet rods.

- We placed a 1-foot-wide bookcase opposite the one that was already part of our bookcase wall. We bolted both cases to the wall and then used two more pipe and flange poles to act as curtain rods. These connected the padded core doors to both bookcases.

- We threaded curtains onto the pipe rods and then screwed them into their flanges mounted at the top corner edges of the far left and the far right bookcases.

- Overhead picture lights on the outside of the closet and lights on the backs of all of the closet shelves made for a great effect at night.

- Inside the closet we used the bookcase shelves for folded clothes, and decorative hatboxes for hidden storage.

AFTER

A Note on Fabric

Nothing says luxury like lots of fabric. But keep it simple, tailored, and solid or textural. The first thing that will date a room is print motifs, so don't lock them into a space where it might be costly to redo.

Window Treatments

You'll notice that in many of our makeovers, we've used wooden blinds instead of fussy, flouncy curtains. This keeps the room looking tailored, and the wood always works well with bookcases. If you want a softer look, use the blinds to control the light, and simply add two stationary fabric panels on each side overlapping the blinds by about an inch.

About the Bed

A lot of times we overlook or try to disguise the bed, especially in small spaces. Don't! The bed should be a focal point to introduce color and luxury to the space. It can be a springboard to a theme, as well. But don't let it overpower a small space. And make sure that when you introduce color, you find ways to incorporate that color throughout the space for visual balance.

To give a glamorous and spacious feeling, we added mirrors to the back-side of the bookcases on either side of the new dining area.

desk to run up both sides of the window, gave the whole unit a great built-in look for little money and little stress. Love that!

Opposite the desk, we took another hollow-core door and cut it into two pieces, one 30 inches and one 56 inches. We then reattached the pieces at a right angle, using the shorter piece as the leg for what would now become the breakfast nook. The longer piece rested on one of the book-case's adjustable shelves—easy, easy. The shelves above were outfitted with dinnerware, a coffeemaker, and even a toaster oven. Cool … I mean hot!

This room illustrates how simple it is to create structure and luxury without needing a carpenter or a loan officer. A myriad of Layer Four (Sort & Contain) issues were beautifully solved by the Design & Build of Layer Five. Layer Six (Arrange & Display) then seemed to almost take care of itself. All thanks to a good beginning with Layer Three and reclaiming space by building rooms within rooms, which not only helps to redefine spaces but stretches space, too. It proves the point: If you can't build out, build up. And when you know how you want your space to function, the rest of the fun is all about getting there.

This is a simple coffee table made from an open-ended plywood box with wheels attached. Four mirror tiles were added to its top and two more to each side to reflect the rest of the space. Two decorative containers keep the inside shelf tidy and well accessorized.

A NOTE ON STORAGE CONTAINERS

Just because you have attractive containers doesn't mean you've got more room for junk. Remember the golden rule: Only store what you really use. If you use it every day, give it the prime real estate. If you use it now and then, work harder to get to it. If you use it once a year, work really hard to get to it. And if you haven't used it in more than a year—*you don't need it!*

TWIN TODDLERS

This toddlers' room takes some of the best ideas you've already seen and adds a whimsical twist with ready-to-assemble furniture and add-on techniques. But this time bold color combines with a very popular, child-friendly theme for a fun and playful look.

The politics of children's rooms, especially if they are shared, is almost as important as the rooms themselves. How you want the children to cohabitate has to be built into the room so that the children feel equal in every way. Whatever one gets, the other had better get, too, or you'll end up with two unhappy campers. Young kids need common, well-defined play areas, but there also needs to be a well-defined study area that lets them know that you mean business. Each child also needs his or her own space, exclusive territory that they are responsible for maintaining and that can be declared off limits. This may also be a "time-out" area.

Before the seven layers of organization were applied, the beds were parallel, not giving the children much privacy. The beds also intruded into the room, cutting down on the common play area. The bookcases lacked contained storage, putting too much pressure on the kids to "display" what they had, and the upper shelves were too high for them to reach. So everyday storage within their reach needed to be pro-

BEFORE

AFTER

vided as well. Because the bookcases were placed along the wall space, there was little room left for artwork by the little Picassos in residence.

With our work cut out for us, our goal was to find a universal kids' theme and really take it over the top. In homage to that classic toy, we chose LEGOs as our theme. The rectangle shapes would be easy to duplicate, and if we were clever, we could use them for storage, too. Even better, the palette of bold primary colors could be just the pick-me-up this space needed. With all that in mind, we purged the space and got to work. We painted the walls yellow—bright and sunny. For the floor we used a same carpet square system, choosing a combination of deep green and light gray to define each child's area with borders and insets. Since we wanted to create some sense of privacy for each child, we kept the beds on the same window wall but placed them lengthwise, foot to foot, with a storage unit in between. Now if both kids were sleeping, they'd at least be out of each other's view. For bed frames, the same IKEA Lack storage units we've used throughout this book were laid parallel on their sides, to support the mattresses. Wicker bins could now be added into each cubbyhole and within reach of each child.

Between the beds we repositioned the existing bookcases back-to-back and perpendicular to the walls. We repeated the arrangement on the opposite side of the room to create the same kind of opening we used in our one-room-living makeover (page 101).

Two large plywood cubes were painted yellow and affixed with "dots" on three sides of the cubes. The dots were made from 1-inch slices of a Styrofoam tube. The cubes were pushed against the back-to-back bookcases. We then built long rectangles out of plywood, affixed dots to each side, painted them blue, and attached them to the sides of the bookcases resting on the top of the yellow base cubes. To top it off, two more square headers, painted yellow and trimmed in the same dots, were attached to the tops of the bookcases and fitted with recessed lights. Opposite each bed, we built a desk for each child using plywood boxes of various shapes and a hollow-core door.

Now, you don't have to be as elaborate, but we wanted to show you how one theme can translate into a variety of projects in a single room. You'll note that the space between the beds and the desk was kept clear for a play area.

I hope this chapter really brings home the point we've been trying to make throughout the book. If you put Layer Five (Design & Build) into action with a few simple yet versatile ready-to-assemble pieces, you can dramatically transform a room. You're limited only by your imagination.

KIDS

CLAIM

Here organization becomes an important part of the room's overall design—it also customizes the space to each child.

RETRO WOW!

In practically every decorating book I've written, my team always tosses in at least one really over-the-top room makeover because we just can't help ourselves. But this is not to say that this retro Barbie room doesn't contain some really cool decorating, display, and storage ideas, because it definitely does.

We wanted to use what was already in the room and add to it. (Hooray for Layer Three, Reclaim & Update!) The bedroom set was a flea-market find or hand-me-down that we dated to the mid-1960s. Its clean lines, raised mitered fronts, and pedestal bases captured our "mod" imagination, and from there we caught the "Barbie's dream house" vision. Knowing that a saturated wall color would create a bold, fresh contrast against these streamlined white pieces, we were determined to have fun.

First, we decided how we'd rearrange the furniture for maximum effect. We liked the white dresser but didn't like that it was the first thing you saw when you entered the room. We wanted to see the groovy new bed, so we moved

BEFORE

AFTER

RIGHT The side tables and the matching bureau were given fresh coats of paint, and the drawer pulls were embellished with craft store moldings. The pedestal legs were accented in light turquoise.

the dresser to the entrance room wall. The next thing we thought about were shapes—curvy shapes and sexy coverings to give the room a more aerodynamic feel and to counter all the square furniture. With a budget between $800 and $1,000 we had to be resourceful, but we still had room for some extravagance. (A chartreuse chintz chair does not come cheap.) The two white suitcases were actually being used for storage, but we needed something to get them off the floor. Lighting was at best hodgepodge, so it went bye-bye. The faux Windsor chair had to go, too, along with its faux early-American attitude—no place for that in go-go-boot land. Now, you could say the same for the Queen Anne writing desk, but its simple curvy legs kept it from getting eighty-sixed.

Once we were through with Layers One and Two, we got out the paint. Choosing a deep yellow chartreuse, we painted the ceiling and the upper three feet of the walls. Continuing the color this way keeps the eye from stopping at the top of the wall and makes the room look taller. To separate one color from the next, we added a very high wainscoting. It and the rest of the trim would be painted dark turquoise. Below this molding we painted the walls bubble-gum pink. While the paint was drying, we tackled our Layer Five furniture projects.

For the bed, we took a lightweight, oval-shaped piece of fiberboard, padded it with batting, and then covered it in chartreuse fabric. This was affixed to the wall hotel-style as a headboard. New linens would customize the rest of the bed.

Sono-tube tuffets were fashioned into cupcake-shaped stools, painted brown, and upholstered in pink fabric over cotton batting. They added whimsy and flexible seating. With a leftover sono-tube we fashioned a mod perfume cabinet by painting it white and adding a round mirror back and glass shelf.

The Queen Anne writing table was also painted white, but it seemed lonely where it was placed. So we purchased two drawer boxes, painted them, and added painted corbels. These then flanked the triple-ringed message center made from three identical picture frames, painted light turquoise, and filled with corkboard off the roll.

Flea-market suitcases grow Queen Anne legs.

A triple ring mirror was made with three identical mirrors, their frames painted turquoise and attached as you see pictured. A simple and easy Reclaim & Update project!

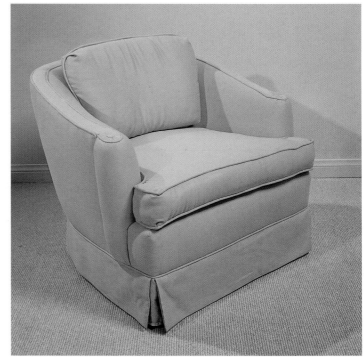

Sublime in lime!

With leftover sono-tube we fashioned a mod perfume cabinet by painting it white and adding a round mirror base and a glass shelf.

Now we're into Layer Six, Arrange & Display. The reupholstered swivel chair arrived, covered in the same fabric as the headboard. It was placed in the opposite corner of the room to disperse the color evenly. Next to it we set a slip-covered cube that matched the upper wall color and brought it down into the lower part of the room. Extending ready-made panels with a new cuff of turquoise fabric gave the window treatments a custom look. The wall-to-wall carpet (saved by Layer Three) simply faded into the background once we added several fake-fur scatter rugs over it.

The accessories and novelty lamps were purchased from mass-market retail outlets and distributed evenly throughout the room. But what really made the room were the round paper lanterns we bought at the local import store. Attached with cup hooks from the ceiling, they looked like a cosmic star cluster. These very inexpensive spheres, done in various sizes but in mass (eighteen total) had a breathtaking effect, especially at night.

While admittedly over-the-top, this room now makes a definite statement that is playful and consistent. Often, we get a good idea but don't have the courage to take it all the way. Remember, if you can't experiment with gleeful abandon in your own home, where can you? Feathering your nest should be fun. Creating a new, streamlined space for your new life should be rewarding. Creating one for your children is even more so. You can do it!

CHECK, PLEASE!

One of the tricks to integrating storage into a room is to make it look built in, or as intentional as possible. If storage units look as though they were always there, the overall design of the room benefits. For example, if everything in the room is stainless steel and you add a white-painted Victorian wicker hutch, it's going to stick out like a sore thumb. While I encourage decorating surprises, it's risky when it comes to storage. If you want to use an old lobster trap with a piece of glass on top in a primitive shore-inspired room, that's one thing—it fits a theme. But as a rule with storage, the less obtrusive, the better.

This is particularly key in kitchens and bathrooms. When I address storage in any room, I try to find an architectural element already in that room to play off of. In this old powder room, for example, I wanted to highlight the black-and-white tiled floor and the black horizontal row of tiles in the bathtub surround. With a $300 budget, we were able to

BEFORE

ENHANCE YOUR VISION

If you can't draw, take a picture of your room. Then sketch over the print to give you a better idea as to how the finished room will look. And don't forget about using descriptive words to unlock your imagination. Words to describe this finished space might be: *streamlined, uniform, uptown, monochromatic, tailored,* and *sophisticated.*

AFTER

LAYERS FIVE AND SIX FOR THE LOO

- To pull the black horizontal strip from the tub area to the other side of the room, we used eight dark steel candle sconces purchased from an import store. They were strategically placed 4 inches apart at the same height as the black ceramic tiles on the other side of the room.

- With a thin piece of molding painted black, we joined the sconces together, creating a handsome single custom unit.

- A black-framed mirror below finished the corner nicely.

- The stacked white toilet paper was just for kicks, but it proves the point that anything can be an accessory. And it's certainly close to where it should be, right?

make tremendous cosmetic changes. And because the room was so small, "building up" was the only option for our Layer Five (Design & Build) plan.

Using 6-inch pine planks, we constructed storage towers to fasten to the right and left of the small sink and close to the tub. To accentuate the black already in the room, we gave the storage towers several coats of high-gloss paint. These would glisten against the newly painted soft gray walls and a darker gray ceiling. The towers enclosing the sink were connected with shelves just above and below the existing mirror. This made the sink surround look built in.

This unit was then filled with decorative bath products and other things a guest might want to use. As Layer Four had us do, we took advantage of glass canisters and liquid dispensers purchased at a bed and bath shop to integrate some of the more commercial and mundane products into the design of the room. The tower by the tub was filled with shampoos, bath salts, and other shower-related products we'd want to be reachable from the inside the tub—more fun and games with Layer Six.

Don't let budget kill your creativity. Once you come up with an idea, look for ways to make what you add to the room look custom built, keeping in mind that consistency and uniformity always work. By closely observing a room and letting it "speak" to you, you'll be surprised at how many clues are there, just waiting for you to find them.

TOWEL RACK TIMES FIVE

The trade-off in gaining lots of storage was that we'd lost the room's only towel rack. To replace it, we took five 2-foot lengths of prethreaded galvanized pipe, ten matching elbows, and ten flanges to secure the pipe to the existing wooden door, leaving enough space between them to accommodate ten fluffy towels, half black and half white, to complement the checkerboard floor.

RESOURCES

Our resource guide has been organized by room and according to my Seven Layers of Design.

SUPER STUDIO
(pages 96–105)

Paint
Sherwin-Williams
Walls: SW 6201, Thunderous Grey

Furniture
Flexsteel/Christopher Lowell Home Collection
IKEA

Fabric Panels
Burlington Coat Factory

Bookcases, Shelves
IKEA

Accessories
Burlington Coat Factory
IKEA
Screwpull

Lighting
LitesNow
Office Depot/Christopher Lowell Office Collection
Robert Abbey

MEALS ON WHEELS
(pages 106–8)

Paint
Christopher Lowell Designer Paint
Walls: Bitter Cocoa
Trim: Arrowroot

Molding
Focal Point Architectural Products

Furniture
IKEA

Blinds
3 Day Blinds/Christopher Lowell Collection

Shelf Unit
IKEA

Hardware
Van Dyke's Restorers

Accessories
Burlington Coat Factory
IKEA
Office Depot

Plants and Trees
Trees International

MEALS ON WHEELS
(pages 110-11)

Paint
Christopher Lowell Designer Paint
Walls: Summer Squash
Trim: Crème Brulée
Sherwin-Williams
Ceiling: SW 6492, Jet Stream

Accent Fabric
Stroheim & Romann

Accessories
Burlington Coat Factory

Plants and Trees
Trees International

SHIP-TO-SHORE BEDROOM, (pages 112–17)

Paint
Sherwin-Williams
Walls: SW 1134, Masterpiece Tan
Trim: White
Ceiling: SW 1226, Winter Cloud

Furniture
Flexsteel/Christopher Lowell Home Collection

Bedding
Burlington Coat Factory/
Christopher Lowell Collection

Bedspread and Pillows
Donna Sayler's Fabulous Furs

Fabric Panels
IKEA

Accessories
IKEA
Umbra

Lighting
Shades of Light

Trees
Trees International

THE SEVEN LAYERS OF DESIGN

Layer 1 Paint & Architecture: moldings, trim, mantels.
Layer 2 Installed Flooring: any floor surface that is wall to wall.
Layer 3 Upholstered Furniture: sofas, love seats, chairs.
Layer 4 Accent Fabrics: area rugs, drapes, pillows, table toppers, runners.
Layer 5 Non-upholstered Furniture: end tables, chairs, coffee tables, desks, bookshelves, armoirs.
Layer 6 Accessories: pictures, mirrors, candlesticks, art.
Layer 7 Plants & Lighting.

For a more detailed explanation of these layers and how to use them, please refer to *Christopher Lowell's Seven Layers of Design: Fearless, Fabulous Decorating*. Now available in paperback at bookstores or online at www.christopherlowell.com

SHIP-TO-SHORE BED-ROOM (pages 118–19)

Paint
Sherwin-Williams
Walls: SW 7017, Dorian Gray
Trim/Ceiling: SW 6386, Napery

Furniture
Flexsteel/Christopher Lowell
Home Collection

Bedding
Burlington Coat Factory/
Christopher Lowell Collection

Lighting
Shades of Light

YACHT CHIC PUBLIC SPACES (pages 120–24)

Paint
Sherwin-Williams
Fireplace Wall: SW 1134
Masterpiece Tan

Furniture and Cushions
Flexsteel/Christopher Lowell
Home Collection

Fabric Panels
IKEA

Accessories
Umbra

Lighting
Shades of Light

YACHT CHIC PUBLIC SPACES (pages 124–25)

Bar Stools
Flexsteel/Christopher Lowell
Home Collection

Cabinet/Piano Top
Bill Newkirk Custom Carpentry

Pillows
Flexsteel/Christopher Lowell
Home Collection

Veneer for Bar Top
Wilson Art

Dimmer and Switch Covers
Lutron Electronics

YACHT CHIC PUBLIC SPACES (page 125)

Bar Stools
Flexsteel/Christopher Lowell
Home Collection

Accessories
Umbra

OFFICE BY DAY, GUEST ROOM BY NIGHT (pages 126–29)

Paint
Sherwin-Williams
Walls: SW 6248, Tubilee
Bead board/Accent: SW 7012,
Creamy

Molding
Focal Point Architectural Products

Tambour
Van Dyke's Restorers

Furniture
Flexsteel/Christopher Lowell
Home Collection

Office Chair
Office Depot/Christopher Lowell
Office Collection

Bedding
Burlington Coat Factory/
Christopher Lowell Collection

Fabric
Calico Corners

Bookcases
IKEA

Hardware
Van Dyke's Restorers

Towels
Burlington Coat Factory/
Christopher Lowell Collection

Accessories
Burlington Coat Factory
IKEA
Office Depot/Christopher Lowell
Office Collection

Lighting
IKEA
Office Depot/Christopher Lowell
Office Collection

Plants and Trees
Trees International

OFFICE POLITICS: DIVIDE AND CONCUR (pages 130–34)

Paint
Sherwin-Williams
Walls: SW 6452, Inland
Trim: White

Molding
Focal Point Architectural Products

Tambour
Van Dyke's Restorers

Furniture
Flexsteel/Christopher Lowell
Home Collection

Office Furniture
Office Depot/Christopher Lowell
Office Collection

Blinds
3 Day Blinds/Christopher Lowell
Collection

Shelves
IKEA

Accessories
IKEA

Lighting
Office Depot/Christopher Lowell
Office Collection
Robert Abbey

Plants and Trees
Office Depot/Christopher Lowell
Office Collection

OFFICE POLITICS: DIVIDE AND CONCUR (page 135)

Paint
Christopher Lowell Designer Paint
Walls: Lowell Lavender

Office Chair
Herman Miller

Fabric
Flexsteel

Desktop Material
Formica Corporation

File Cabinet
McDowell Craig Office Furniture

Accessories
Burlington Coat Factory
Cost Plus World Market
IKEA

Lighting
IKEA

PASS-THROUGH SPACES: THE LONG HALL
(pages 136–39)

Paint
Shelves: Shellac
Trim: Black

Adhesive
Liquid Nails

Accessories
Burlington Coat Factory
IKEA
Loose Ends

PASS-THROUGH SPACES: THE LONG HALL
(pages 140–41)

Paint
Christopher Lowell Designer Paint
Walls: Summer Squash
Trim: Arrowroot
Ceiling: Vanilla Mist

Anaglypta (Wall Treatment)
Van Dyke's Restorers

Accessories
Burlington Coat Factory
IKEA
Pier 1 Imports

Lighting
Robert Abbey

COLLEGE COOL
(pages 142–47)

Paint
Sherwin-Williams
Walls: SW 6192, Coastal Plain
Trim: White

Furniture
Office Depot/Christopher Lowell
Office Collection

Bedding
Burlington Coat Factory/
Christopher Lowell Collection

Blinds
3 Day Blinds/Christopher Lowell
Collection

Bookcases
IKEA

Accessories
Burlington Coat Factory
IKEA

SORORITY SPLENDOR
(pages 148–53)

Paint
Sherwin-Williams
Walls: SW 6010, Flexible Gray

Furniture
IKEA

Desk Chair
Office Depot/Christopher Lowell
Office Collection

Fabric Panels
Burlington Coat Factory

Bedding
Burlington Coat
Factory/Christopher Lowell
Collection

Blinds
3 Day Blinds

CD Shelves
IKEA

Accessories
Burlington Coat Factory
IKEA

Lighting
IKEA

Trees
Trees International

TWIN TODDLERS
(pages 154–59)

Paint
Christopher Lowell Designer Paint
Walls: Curried Mango
Trim: White

Tesserae Carpet System
Milliken Carpet & Rugs

Area Rug, Bookcases, Matress
IKEA

Blinds
3 Day Blinds

Accessories, Lighting, Shelving Units
IKEA

RETRO WOW!
(pages 160–65)

Paint
Sherwin-Williams
Top of Walls: SW 6918, Humorous
Green
Bottom of Walls: SW 6977, Queenly
Trim/Accent: SW 6945, Belize

Corbels, Hardware, Wooden Legs for Suitcases
Van Dyke's Restorers

Accessories
Burlington Coat Factory
IKEA

Lighting
IKEA

CHECK, PLEASE!
(pages 166–69)

Paint
Christopher Lowell Designer Paint
Walls: Blue Points
Trim: Dried Blueberry Dust
Ceiling: Huckleberry Dust
Accent: Black

Quilted Metal
Frigo Design

Towels
Burlington Coat
Factory/Christopher Lowell
Collection

Candle Sconces
Illuminations

Accessories, Lighting
IKEA

CONTACT INFORMATION

Alpha Productions
310-559-1364
www.alphaproductions.com

Antique Drapery Rod Company
214-653-1733
www.antiquedraperyrod.com

Art Select
888-686-4254
www.artselect.com

Bendheim Architectural Glass
212-226-6370
www.bendheim.com

Bill Newkirk Custom Carpentry
818-566-1608

Blik Surface Graphics
866-262-BLIK (2545)
www.whatisblik.com

Burlington Coat Factory
800-444-2628
www.coat.com

Burlington Coat
Factory/Christopher Lowell
Collection
800-444-2628
www.christopherlowell.com

Calico Corners
800-213-6366
www.calicocorners.com

Christopher Lowell Designer Paint
www.christopherlowell.com

Christopher Lowell's Color
Courage Kit
www.christopherlowell.com

Cost Plus World Market
510-893-7300
www.costplus.com

Diverse Imaging
949-498-9940
www.diverseimaging.com

DMI Furniture
877-831-0319
www.dmifurniture.com

Donna Sayler's Fabulous Furs
800-848-4650
www.fabulousfurs.com

Douglas Hill Photography
323-660-0681
www.doughill.com

Flexsteel
800-685-7632
www.flexsteel.com

Flexsteel/Christopher Lowell
Home Collection
800-685-7632
www.christopherlowell.com

Focal Point Architectural Products
800-662-5550
www.focalpointap.com

Formica Corporation
800-FORMICA (367-6422)
www.formica.com

Frigo Design
800-836-8746
www.frigodesign.com

Herman Miller
888-443-4357
www.hermanmiller.com

IKEA
800-434-IKEA (4532)
www.ikea.com

Illuminations
800-621-2998
www.illuminations.com

Inova
866-528-2804
www.inovallc.com

Liquid Nails
800-634-0015
www.liquidnails.com

LitesNow
800-945-4837
www.litesnow.com

Loose Ends
503-390-7457
www.looseends.com

Lutron Electronics
888-LUTRON 1 (588-7661)
www.lutron.com

McDowell Craig Office Furniture
877-921-2100
www.mcdowellcraig.com

Milliken Carpet & Rugs
800-241-8666
www.millikencarpet.com

Office Depot
800-463-3768
www.officedepot.com

Office Depot/Christopher Lowell
Office Collection
800-463-3768
www.christopherlowell.com

Pier 1 Imports
800-245-4595
www.pier1.com

Robert Abbey
828-322-3480
www.robertabbey.com

Rowenta
781-396-0600
www.rowenta.com

Screwpull
877-CREUSET (273-8738)
www.lecreuset.com

Shades of Light
800-262-6612
www.shadesoflight.com

Sherwin-Williams
888-686-4254
www.sherwin-williams.com

Stroheim & Romann
718-706-7000
www.stroheim.com

Sunbrella
336-227-6211
www.sunbrella.com

3 Day Blinds/Christopher Lowell
Collection
800-800-3329
www.3day.com

Trees International
888-873-3799
www.treesinternational.com

Umbra
800-387-5122
www.umbra.com

Van Dyke's Restorers
800-558-1234
www.vandykes.com

Wilson Art
800-433-3222
www.wilsonart.com

ACKNOWLEDGMENTS

I would like to thank so many people who contributed directly and indirectly to one of the most important books we've ever produced. First of all, to our readers and viewers, thank you for sharing your honest insights and dilemmas with us over the years. Without your input this book would not be nearly as effective in helping you truly make your home that wonderful reflection of who you are and, more important, who you say you want to become.

Behind this book is an extraordinary and talented team of experts who had also taken your desire to unclutter your life seriously. To Frances Schultz, my editor, for helping me organize this weighty material while keeping it easy to read, inspiring, and effective. To my creative team, Jocelyne Borys, Michael Murphy, and their crews, thank you for your hard work, candor, and dedication to helping me continue to establish how America will look and live in the future. To Douglas Hill, our ever-flexible photographer, who pictorially captured our efforts so beautifully. To my financial staff, Shelly Gates, Gerri Leonard, and her team at Sendyk Leonard & Co., for stretching and tracking the budgets so that it all shows on the pages. To my corporate team, headed by Daniel J. Levin—thank you. And to Todd Optican, Sohayla Cude, and Marie Fitch for keeping the big machine running like a top. To Janet Newell and Laura Madden McBride, who work on the front lines, getting all of our viewers' questions answered on a daily basis while continuing to supply them with up-to-date content to help them feather their nests. To my business partners, Office Depot, Flexsteel, 3 Day Blinds, and Burlington Coat Factory, along with various vendors who contribute to many of the furnishings depicted in our photos.

And finally, to my Clarkson Potter team of Lauren Shakely, Pam Krauss, Aliza Fogelson, Maggie Hinders, Caitlin Daniels Israel, Sibylle Kazeroid, Rosy Ngo, and Tammy Blake, who continue to keep me in the publishing forefront—thank you for helping us continually get first-rate products out to my loyal readers. And to my PR team at BWR, Ron Hofmann, and Hayley Scheck, for keeping America informed about all our goings-on. Together my many associates and I remain committed to helping contribute to the quality of your lives, and we thank you for the opportunity to help make a difference.

INDEX

A

apartment, studio, 96–105
appliances, 28–29, 51–53
attics, 58

B

banquettes, 109, 110, 123
baskets, 50, 115
bathroom storage ideas, 48–49,
    58, 166–69
bedrooms. *See also* beds
    guest rooms, 37, 118, 126–29
    master, 112–19
    retro-style, 160–65
    storage ideas, 50
    teenage boy's, 142–47
    teenage girl's, 148–53
    twin toddlers', 154–59
beds
    backrest for, 128
    daybeds, 37, 147
    drapery panels for, 80
    elevating, 147
    as focal point, 151
    placement of, 157
    retro-style, 162
    storage ideas, 57, 66, 102, 112,
        113–14, 115, 117, 118, 147, 157
bills, 89
blankets, 27, 50
bookcases
    backs of, 67
    choosing, 64–69
    configuring, ideas for, 38
    dividing space with, 85, 104, 134,
        157
    doors for, 69
    encasing furniture with, 102
    encasing workspace with, 38,
        64, 65, 129, 148, 152
    hardware for, 69

    with no back, 67
    professional installers for, 64
    shelves for, 67–69
books, 26, 50, 90
breakfast nooks, 110–11, 152
budgets, 62, 99
bulk purchases, 54, 89

C

cabinets, medicine, 27
canisters, 58
cars, 88
cell phones, 26
charitable organizations, 31
china, 29
closets, 39, 50, 144, 150
clothing
    discarding, 28, 89
    keepsake, 34
    storing, 39, 50, 115, 117, 144, 150
clutter
    discarding, 30–31
    identifying, 26–29, 87
    minimizing, strategies for, 88–91
    pack rat profiles, 14–18
color groups, 76–77
computers, 26, 88
consignment shops, 31
containers. *See* storage containers
cosmetics, 27

D

daybeds, 37, 147
decorative objects, 33–34
desks, 116, 135, 144, 148, 152, 156–57,
    162–63
dining areas
    breakfast nooks, 108–9, 152
    increasing seating in, 106–11
    piano "table" in, 123, 125
    storage ideas for, 51–54, 106–11

dishwashers, 89
display techniques and tips
    allowing empty spaces, 80
    in bathrooms, 48–49, 58
    glass containers for, 48, 58, 169
    grouping, by colors, 76–77
    grouping, by objects, 73–75
    grouping, by themes, 78–79
    in kitchens, 46, 58
    with lifts and levels, 77
domino effect, 30, 91

E

eBay, 31

F

fabric, 151
fax machines, 26
fear of change, 12, 43, 61, 85
flatware, 29
floors, 139
food storage, 46, 53
furniture. *See also specific types*
    buying, advice for, 63–64
    discarding, 35–37
    rearranging, 63, 82
    reevaluating need for, 34–37
    in small spaces, 82

G

garages, 58
garage sales, 31
glass containers, 48, 58, 169
glass shelves, 68, 69, 104
grocery shopping, 89
guest rooms, 37, 118–19, 126–29

H

hair products, 27
hallways, 39, 136–41
hatbox collections, 75

home offices
    in guest room, 126–29
    shared by two people, 130–35
    storage ideas for, 50, 134
    workstations, 39, 65, 102, 129,
        148, 152

J

junk, identifying, 23, 26–29

K

kitchens, 28–29, 46, 51–54, 58,
    124

L

lamps, 34, 40, 125
lanterns, 165
laundry, 89
lifts and levels, 77
lighting, 85
    lamps, 34, 40, 125
    lanterns, 165
    track lights, 83–84, 100
    wall sconces, 110, 133
linens
    bathroom, 27, 46, 48–49, 54
    bed, 27, 54
    table, 29, 53
living rooms, 50, 96–98, 101–2,
    123

M

magazine holders, 50, 135
magazines, 88
mail, junk, 89
medicine cabinets, 27
mirrors, 140, 164
mirror tiles, 67, 139
monochromatic scheming,
    76–77
mudrooms, 58

N

newspapers, 26

O

office supplies, 47, 54

ottomans, 40

P

paperwork, 26, 27

phone books, 90

phones, cell, 26

pillows, 50

place mats, 29, 53

postcard collections, 73

pot racks, 124

pots and pans, 29, 51–53

pottery collections, 76

projects

    bathroom storage unit, 169

    closet/desk unit, 144

    curtain closet and headboard, 150

    custom bookcases, 104

    dining area banquette, 109

    elevated daybed, 147

    framed wall sconces, 110

    hallway shelves, 137–39

    sliding desk over bed, 116

    sono-tube coffee table, 128

towel rack, 169

workstation, 129

work surface/storage unit, 134

purging process

    discarding clutter, 29–31

    discarding junk, 26–29

    psychological fear of, 43

    as a way of life, 87–91

S

scanners, 88

sconces, 110, 133

seating

    banquette, 109, 110, 123

    hallway, 139

    living room, 82, 96–98

Seven Layers of Organization, summary of, 92–93

shelving, 67–69, 104, 133, 137–39

slipcovers, 34

small spaces, 82

sofas, 34–37, 96–97, 102

sono-tube table, 128

spoon collections, 73

storage containers

    for bulk purchases, 54

    buying, advice for, 59, 63

    canisters, 58

    cloth-lined, 58

    as design element, 63, 105

    glass, 48, 58, 169

    identical, grouping together, 73, 74

    lids for, 56

    limiting number of, 90, 153

    metal and enamel, 56

    see-through, 56

    shapes for, 56

storage ideas

    bathroom, 48–49, 58, 166–69

    bedroom, 50, 57, 66, 102, 113–14, 116–18, 147, 157

    clothing, 39, 50, 144, 149

    concealed, 46–47

    dining area, 51–54

    home office, 50, 134

    kitchen, 46, 51–54, 58, 124

    living room, 50, 101–2, 123

    utility room, 50

studio apartment, 96–105

suitcases, 40, 162

T

tablecloths, 53

tables

    alternatives to, 40–42

coffee, 40, 42, 82, 128, 146

dining area, 37, 107, 109, 123, 125, 152

kitchen, 124

painting, 105

tax records, 26, 27

toiletries, 48, 169

tools, 50

towel racks, 169

towels, 27, 46, 48–49, 54, 169

track lighting, 83–84, 100

trash removal services, 31

U

utility areas, 58

utility rooms, 50

W

wall colors, 99, 128, 132, 140, 162

warehouse clubs, 54

wastebaskets, 88

windows, 110, 133

window treatments, 81, 115, 127, 133, 151

wineglasses, 29

wood, laminated, 69

workstations, 39, 64–65, 129, 148, 152.

    See also home offices